FOLLOW THE MOON

.10

First published in 2006 by
CURRACH PRESS
55A Spruce Avenue, Stillorgan Industrial Park, Blackrock, Co. Dublin

www.currach.ie

1 3 5 4 2

Cover by Sin é Design
Origination by Currach Press
Printed by ColourBooks, Baldoyle Industrial Estate, Dublin 13
ISBN: 1-85607-942-2

The author and publishers are grateful to the following for permission to reproduce copyright material:

Little, Brown and Company for an excerpt from Jimmy Breslin's memoir, *I Want to Thank My Brain for Remembering Me*; Kiepenheuer & Witsch for parts of two letters from *Rom auf den ersten Blick* by Heinrich Böll © 1989 by Verlag Kiepenheuer & Witsch, Köln, translated from the German by Leila Vennewitz; the Society of Authors as the literary representative of the estate of A. E. Housman for XVIII from *Last Poems* by A. E. Housman; *Irish Times* Photo Editor Peter Thursfield for the back cover photo taken by Alan Betson in 2000; and the *Boston Globe* for the obituary of Mary Elizabeth Sullivan written by Kevin Cullen.

The sections on Jimmy Breslin, Heinrich Böll, John Moriarty and living in Achill evolved from pieces first published in *The Irish Times*. An extract from the chapter 'Letter from Norman' was published in *A Century of Service, Muintir Mhaigh Eo, Áth Cliath, 1905–2005*, edited by Christy Loftus.

FOLLOW THE MOON

A MEMOIR

SHEILA SULLIVAN

CURRACH PRESS

Acknowledgements

Thanks to Jo O'Donoghue for her immediate response to the manuscript, and to Sinéad McKenna for designing the cover. Eoin McVey and Liam Ryan of *The Irish Times* agreed to the unpaid leave during which I finished writing this book.

René Böll shared his family history without hesitation.

Special thanks to Jimmy Breslin and Ronnie Eldridge, John Moriarty, Jonathan Williams, John Banville, Peter Thursfield, David Langston, Francis Oakley, Mary Dixon, John Behan, Joe Papin, Tom Honeyman, Karin Sullivan Killeen, Kevin Cullen, Michael O'Mahony, Esther Murnane, John Butler, the Achill Heinrich Böll Association and all those on both sides of the Atlantic who answered my questions, revived memories and helped check facts.

Thanks most of all to my son Conor, my husband Brent and my parents, Frederick Joseph Sullivan (1914–81) and Mary Elizabeth Sullivan (1926–94).

For Brent and Conor

Contents

'It has a stark beauty all its own. It's like much of the high desert of the United States. It's different but it's very pretty out here.'
– Astronaut Neil Armstrong, while walking on the moon, 20 July 1969

I

DEATH OF A NEWSMAN

Father Patrick Monahan was getting ready to go running when the phone rang in his Dún Laoghaire home. The parish priest of St Michael's, he was in training for the Paris marathon and he looked forward to a long run in the January air. He answered the phone and listened for a few moments.

'Fine. Do you have a number for the family?'

He jotted down a mobile number and said, 'Thank you,' then hung up. He made a note that the regular ten o'clock Mass on Wednesday morning would be a funeral. He wanted to think about his homily while he ran. The caller had said the deceased man's former wife and son would arrive on the Castlebar–Dublin train on Tuesday evening. He would ring their mobile number then.

Mrs Norah Owens was trying to finish a jumper she had been knitting for forty years when the phone rang in her Sandycove home. She put aside her knitting needles and wool and got up from her chair to answer it. The caller told her that a man she had befriended over the past few years had died at Carlisle Terrace, on Tivoli Road. She was shocked and sad. A fine man, she thought, well dressed, always gentlemanly to her. He was American and had been a newspaperman. She thanked the caller and put down the phone. Norah dialled the number of her daughter-in-law,

9

Joan Dalton, and told her the news. Norah said she thought that the man who died might have had something to do with Joan's friend in Achill, who was also an American journalist. Joan asked Norah the name of the deceased man and then gasped in recognition. She said she would phone her friend. Norah offered to help with arrangements in any way that she could, and then she said goodbye.

I had worked from Wednesday to Friday in the newsroom of *The Irish Times* and had taken the train from Heuston Station to Castlebar on Saturday morning as usual. The train had stopped for a long time in Ballyhaunis and I was tired; after many months of commuting between Dublin and Mayo I was beginning to feel like a chimpanzee in space. When I arrived in Achill I went for a walk on Dugort beach with Brent and Conor to clear my head and shake off the city and the train. It was 4 January 2003 and the day was clear and cold. Brent and I stood on the beach and looked at Blacksod Bay while Conor ran along the shore.

My answering machine was blinking with messages when I got home at 5:25 pm. The calls were all from Joan, my American friend who was living in Killiney; she sounded tense. In one message she told me to go upstairs to my office and to phone her from there. My chest felt tight when I rang her.

'Are you in your little office upstairs?' Joan asked.

'Yes.'

There was a silence.

'Sheila, Bob died.'

Joan said her mother-in-law had got the call notifying her of his death; Norah and Joan had not wanted me to hear the news from the police. I paused momentarily to marvel at the fact that, in a city of a million people, Bob and I had become close to different branches of the same family. Norah was offering to help with funeral arrangements, and Joan gave me her mother-in-law's number. I said Bob's family in America would have to be contacted. He had a sister in Long Beach Island, New Jersey, who was thirteen years older. I stifled a sob.

'There's a room for you here,' Joan said. She gave me the phone number of the garda sergeant who had found Bob and another one for the undertaker who had been contacted by the garda sergeant. I thanked her and hung up.

I went downstairs and knocked on the door of Conor's bedroom. He was eleven years old. I climbed up on to the top bunk-bed, something I never did, and sat down and told him that his father had died. His large brown eyes were wide as I spoke. 'Is it okay if I cry?' he asked.

'Of course.' I hugged him and we said a prayer for his father. I stayed on the top bunk-bed with Conor while we tried to absorb the shock. I told him that I hadn't brought him into the world to feel such pain. Then I said I had to make some phone calls and went back upstairs to my office.

Brent went into Conor's room and told him that he loved him. It was pitch-dark now and cold outside in Achill.

I phoned the garda sergeant and gave him a number for Noreen, in America, and asked him to ring her with the news. Bob and I had been divorced in 1997, his parents were long dead and he had no other close family except cousins in Cork. I said I would help with arrangements if Noreen wanted. I hung up and went back downstairs to Conor.

The phone rang soon afterwards. It was the sergeant. 'I'm sorry, but I rang the number you gave me for Bob's sister,' he said, 'and was told that she is dead. She died of lung cancer six weeks ago, her husband said.'

'May I see him?' I asked the undertaker. Bob's body was in the morgue in Loughlinstown.

'No.'

'Why not?'

'The coroner won't permit it.'

'The sergeant phoned Bob's sister in America,' I said, 'and found out that she is dead.'

'Oh my God.'

'What happens now?'

'He'll go to a pauper's grave,' the undertaker said.

My head was swimming and my chest was tight. The phrase 'pauper's grave' shot through me like a bullet from a gun.

'No,' I told the undertaker. 'No.' I told him to purchase a grave in Shanganagh Cemetery, which is beside the sea, not too far from where we had lived in Dalkey when Conor was a baby. I would take charge of the funeral arrangements. Bob's friend Norah would help me with the planning. He could send the bill to me.

I went downstairs and climbed back on top of Conor's bunk-bed. My chest hurt now. I told him that his aunt had died and that we would organise the funeral for his dad in Dublin. Did he think he would be able to read something short at the funeral? He said he wasn't sure. I said he didn't have to decide at that moment.

My mind raced with grief and horror and responsibility. I phoned Father Paddy Gilligan, the parish priest in Achill Sound, and asked to see him, and he immediately made himself available. He suggested a reading from the New Testament if Conor was able, and he gave me a booklet containing selections for funeral Masses. He was a mannerly, well-spoken man from Ballintubber, County Mayo, who reminded me of a young Rod Steiger.

'Thank you for seeing me.'

'It's been a privilege.'

When I got home from the priest's house I clutched Bob's New York press pass, allowing the bearer to get through police lines wherever formed. In the laminated photo he was a handsome, hazel-eyed young man with the long hair of the 1970s who bore a strong resemblance to the writer Sebastian Barry, although he was no relation.

Bob, whose full name was Robert Michael Barry Lane, was born in 1946 in New York, the son of James Lane and Mary Barry from Cork city. He was educated at St John's University and Fordham. He entered Dunwoodie, formally known as St Joseph's Seminary, in Yonkers, New York, but left before becoming a priest.

In 1969 he was hired by the *New York Daily News* when it was a big, brash tabloid that had more than one million readers and was so confident that when President Gerald Ford refused to bail out the Big Apple during a financial crisis, the paper ran the headline: 'Ford to City: Drop Dead'. Bob stayed at the *News* for seventeen years as a reporter, rewrite man and assistant night city editor. In the 1980s he became assistant to the editor, F. Gilman Spencer, former editor of the Philadelphia *Daily News* and winner of the 1974 Pulitzer Prize for editorial writing at the *Trentonian* in New Jersey.

Bob reported, wrote and edited thousands of stories about the people and the city of New York. He covered the trial of serial killer David Berkowitz, the so-called 'Son of Sam' or '44-calibre killer' who murdered six people and terrorised New Yorkers in 1976 and 1977 before finally being apprehended by police over a parking ticket he received at the scene of his final crime.

I have an old clip from the *Daily News* from 23 May 1978 bearing the headline 'Berkowitz Goes Wild in Court' by Robert Lane and Alton Slagle. Berkowitz went berserk at his sentencing hearing in Brooklyn Supreme Court and tried to jump out the window. He had broken away from guards and tried to plunge from a seventh-floor window on to Court Street. The fracas left one court officer hospitalised and another injured. His sentencing was delayed.

Bob told me that while he looked on in court David Berkowitz had screamed, 'That's her! That's her! I'll kill them all!' at Neysa Moskowitz, the mother of his final victim, Stacy Moskowitz.

'You animal!' Mrs Moskowitz had screamed, and rushed from the chamber in tears. The Son of Sam serial killer eventually was sentenced to six life sentences.

I knew Bob's byline before I knew him, and thought he wrote clearly under the pressure of a daily deadline. He was almost ten years older than myself and at the time much more experienced in journalism. He was quirky and humorous and he had a light touch on the keyboard when required. A beauty contestant was accused of padding her bra for the swimsuit section of the competition and Bob was sent to interview her. His report began: 'With a red, white and blue sash across her shapely but controversial chest ...'

We had spoken on the phone a couple of times. He was on the desk when I covered the Irish protest against the ill-timed visit of Prince Charles to Lincoln Center during the 1981 Maze hunger strikes. It was a warm summer evening in Manhattan. The royal party arrived in their limousines, resplendent in formal attire. Outside, protesters, who included relatives of the hunger-strikers, were standing on the back of a flatbed truck, non-violent but angry. I was on a pay phone in a crowd of five thousand people, near a group of Irish protesters who were banging the lids of rubbish bins on the ground. My seersucker dress was soaked with sweat. I had just got a good story: a New York City police officer of Irish descent who had been protecting the prince had gone home to take off his uniform and had returned in civilian clothes to demonstrate against Charles's visit. He was willing to talk to me.

'I don't have time to chat,' Bob said when I phoned the city desk, intending to check in and then dictate my notes to a rewrite man.

'I don't chat,' I said to Bob, and hung up. I rang the *News* again, got the switchboard and asked to speak directly to the rewrite man.

After that we shared a double byline on the story of a verdict in an arson trial in Brooklyn and we finally met in the newsroom when I was working nights in Manhattan. As I recall, we were not introduced. He was standing near the news desk, a six-foot-four, handsome young man with dark-brown hair, wearing a green jumper and smoking a cigarette. He said he heard that I had lived in Ireland and told me he wanted to move there.

We were married about two years later.

He had a beautiful baritone voice. Briefly a member of the St Patrick's Cathedral choir in New York, he sang with the choir at Cardinal Cooke's funeral in October 1983. The lights of St Patrick's had stayed on all night as the cardinal lay dying in his residence behind the Gothic-style cathedral. Bob and I had been married for six months and were living across from St Patrick's at the time. 'I think the cardinal died,' Bob said the following morning, and I wondered how he knew. Then I heard the bells tolling.

We had come to Ireland in 1986 to work for an American journalist, Martin O'Shea, who had been publishing a newspaper, *Ireland Digest*, aimed at an American readership. I had read a news item about him in *The New York Times*, where he had worked. He had produced some good-looking issues of the paper and he had offered Bob a contract for one year. I was hoping to do some freelance journalism for *Ireland Digest* and begin to research and write a book while we got settled. We thought Bob's position would tide us over for while.

Bob left his job as assistant to the editor of the *Daily News* and I left mine as writer-producer in CNN's New York bureau, and we rented a house in Spiddal, County Galway, where the paper was supposed to be based.

''Tis a grand view you have, but I'm not sure 'tis a paradise you've come to,' the moving man said to me, eyeing me gravely.

Ireland Digest proved to be a short-lived, ill-fated venture. After a month or so we parted company with Martin O'Shea when we correctly surmised that there would be no more issues of the newspaper.

'What are you going to *do*?' an American journalist who worked in Ireland asked. Many Irish journalists helped, providing names, phone numbers and contacts at all the major news organisations in Dublin. I was thirty years old; Bob was almost forty. It was September 1986, and thirty thousand people were leaving Ireland each year, some handing keys to their houses to bank managers on the way to the airport. But we were very determined. We read the appointments sections of the papers and wrote letters on a big, old, manual Royal typewriter, a goodbye present from the *Daily News*. We had no phone. I remember running up the driveway of the house in Spiddal in my dressing gown, chasing a Telecom Éireann van as it drove along the coast road, begging the man to come to the house and connect the line. He actually responded to my plea.

In December Bob was called to an interview at the GPO for the position of Advertising and Public Relations Manager of the National Lottery, which was (and still is) run by An Post. He went to Dublin by train, wearing his best suit from New York. He was interviewed by a panel led by a man who, Bob said, looked like Éamon de Valera. When I collected him at the train station in Galway, he said, 'I think they only had me in for a laugh.'

'They just phoned. They want you back next week for another interview,' I told him.

He got the job and we moved to Dublin, where I began my job search. We stayed for many weeks in a large spare bedroom in a house Tom MacIntyre was renting on Upper Beechwood Avenue, Ranelagh, across the street from what the writer called 'the Walt Disney church'. I had met Tom in 1977 at Williams College in Massachusetts and we had become great friends. When Bob and I arrived in Ireland, Tom was collaborating with the artistic director of the Abbey Theatre, Patrick Mason, and actor Tom Hickey on his theatrical adaptation of Patrick Kavanagh's poem *The Great Hunger*. We saw the play at the Peacock in July 1986 and attended an astonishing show in the barnyard at Annaghmakerrig, County Monaghan, in August of that year. The production toured the world, winning a Fringe First Award in Edinburgh, receiving a rapturous response in Paris in 1987 and mixed and turbulent ones in Moscow and New York in 1988.

The house on Upper Beechwood was heated by pellets of solid fuel that were kept in a container in the back garden, a situation which amazed a couple of New Yorkers used to push-button living. There was a contraption in the kitchen, a boiler, which MacIntyre called 'Baby', and although Baby sometimes gave trouble, Bob soon mastered its idiosyncrasies. 'Time to feed Baby,' Tom would call in his carrying voice when the boiler needed more solid fuel.

Job-hunting in the Dublin journalism world in the winter of 1986 and spring of 1987 was difficult and discouraging. Though I was treated immaculately, the opportunities were not there. When I returned to Upper Beechwood Avenue after pounding the pavements, Tom would sometimes say: 'Go on. Give us a bit of your Beckett,' and I'd recite one line from *Waiting for Godot*, when Vladimir says:

> But it is not for nothing I have lived through this
> long day and I can assure you it is very near the end
> of its repertory.

Tom would laugh and shout his approval, and I'd take heart. Without his encouragement and his roof over our heads we could not have stayed in Ireland.

In July 1987 I was hired as a staff sub-editor in *The Irish Times*, and with Bob at the Lottery the future looked brighter. By that point we were renting an apartment in Sandymount, Dublin.

Bob played a key role in the successful start-up of the National Lottery but he missed the newspaper business and he moved to *The Irish Times*, where he was hired as a revise editor, a new position at the time. For some years he settled into the routine with an almost military discipline, but it was not to last. He wasn't happy and he wasn't well: his dependence on alcohol was taking a terrible toll. After I initiated a separation in 1994, he began taking medication for depression. His hospitalisations were numerous and his deterioration was frightening and painful to observe. He was unable to work. He died suddenly over the Christmas period early in 2003, shortly after his fifty-sixth birthday. His death certificate, which I collected from an office in Dún Laoghaire with a shaking hand, said the cause of death was acute respiratory compromise, bilateral pulmonary embolism, source not found.

He grew up in Washington Heights in New York City, the son of Irish immigrants. His parents left Cork separately in the 1920s, marrying later in the US; both had travelled by ship to America and gone through Ellis Island. In the summer Bob's mother took him back to Ireland by ship and he swam in the sea in Skibbereen. Despite long years in America, the Cork ties remained strong. Christy Ring stayed overnight in Bob's New York home, and Jack Lynch visited the Lanes in the United States before he became Taoiseach.

His life was shattered when his mother, a radiological technician at Columbia Presbyterian Hospital, died of breast cancer, aged fifty-eight, when he was sixteen. His father eventually returned to Cork, where he died aged eighty.

Over the years there were stories from Ireland. One involved a letter received from a Donegal woman who had worked for a family on Park Avenue and retired to Ireland to look after a mildly-disabled younger relative. 'Here I am, living up here with this nitwit,' the letter began. When the older woman died, the story goes, the younger woman ran through the house in Donegal waving a green-and-white document and wailing: 'Who's going to pay the television licence? Who's going to pay the television licence?'

Another story came from 1950s Cork. Bob's sister was on a bus when a man patted the breast pocket of his jacket.

'Do you know what I have in me pocket?' he asked her.

She didn't know what to say.

He smiled at her and patted his pocket again. 'A bone for me dog.'

'Mum, that woman just blessed herself,' Conor said. We were in a black limousine, following the hearse. Conor was right; people standing at a bus stop in Dún Laoghaire were blessing themselves as the hearse passed. It was 8 January 2003.

As we approached St Michael's, I saw a colleague cross Marine Road; with his tall frame and long trench coat, he looked like Bob. I looked at Dún Laoghaire harbour, where a ferry was leaving for Holyhead. The sea was a little choppy, the sky was slightly overcast, but there was no wind or rain. *Fuair sé dea-lá chun na cille.* He had good weather for his funeral. I looked back at St Michael's and saw a group of colleagues waiting on the steps outside the church. Conor and I got out of the limousine and the journalists, most of whom either had not seen him since he was a baby or had never met him, smiled.

Father Monahan came outside and asked if I had Conor's reading. I did. He spoke quickly and I had trouble keeping up with what he was saying. He asked me for a list of people who would speak and I handed him a piece of paper. First reading from the Old Testament: Denis Kirwan, who had worked with Bob at the Lottery; second reading from the New Testament: son Conor; prayers of the faithful: Norah Owens; offertory gifts: cousin Denis Barry from Cork and son Conor; eulogy: former wife Sheila. He asked me for two or three words that would describe Bob.

'A good newsman'.

We entered the church, which I had never seen. The organ was in the front; the pulpit looked like Ogham stones. There was a large crowd inside and all stood up as we entered. My head went back slightly, listening to the music and the rumbling sound of the congregation standing up. Bob's gigantic cousins, Barrys from Cork city who were well over six feet tall, like Bob himself, had arrived that morning at the funeral home to carry the coffin, and

Conor was helping them now.

I watched in wonder as the priest, singer and organist acted in concert; the singer sounded at times like Bob. *How great thou art*, he sang. *Be not afraid. Amazing grace, how sweet the sound.* The Christmas decorations were still up; there were camels on the altar.

The undertaker had handed me a booklet for the bereaved. It said: 'Sometimes, in the early stages of grief, you may think you "see" him or her – on the street, in a bus, getting into a car.'

There were more people in the church than I had expected. We had arrived in Ireland in 1986 knowing almost no one apart from Bob's relatives in Cork and Tom MacIntyre in Dublin. My eyes tried to take in the faces of friends, former neighbours, many of Bob's former co-workers at the National Lottery and a strong contingent of our colleagues from *The Irish Times*, including the former editor, Conor Brady, and the new editor, Geraldine Kennedy, nicknamed 'Madam' because for the first time in the newspaper's history letters to the editor began 'Dear Madam' instead of 'Dear Sir'.

'I didn't know you knew so many people, Mum,' my son said.

As we sat in the front pew, a little to the right of Bob's flower-covered coffin, the memory of my late parents hung over my shoulders, protecting me like an invisible shield.

Father Monahan, it turned out, was a quick study and he had an Irish genius for funerals. He mentioned Bob's name several times during the Mass and referred to him as a good newsman. He remembered Noreen in prayers. He gave a highly intelligent homily on the case for life after death: looking directly at me, he argued that if there were nothing else, it would negate everything we held to be meaningful in this life. He prayed that there would be no invasion of Iraq.

I had met him for the first time the night before in the Royal Marine Hotel, Dún Laoghaire. Intense and kind, in his early fifties with reddish-grey hair, he was born in Maynooth, County

Kildare. He had run fifteen marathons from Belfast to Beijing, writing sermons in his head while he ran. I assumed that running provided an outlet for his intensity. He had just returned from a sabbatical year in California, where he had done a master's degree in post-modern philosophy at Berkeley and had taken a course on Suffering. Many people thought I had chosen him and must have known him for years but that was not the case. He was there because Bob had died in his parish, yet he was the perfect person to conduct Bob's funeral. I asked Father Monahan if there were any books which could help me, and he suggested *A Grief Observed* by C. S. Lewis and *Working on God* by Winifred Gallagher, a former reporter.

When Father Monahan called Conor to the altar to give the second reading from the New Testament, you could hear a pin drop in the church. I never took my eyes off my son, as though somehow that might help him. Should I have asked him to do this? I waited and watched. The congregation seemed to hold its collective breath. Then Conor began reading from the first letter of St John as though he had been reading at funerals all his life. He was concentrating hard, his brown hair and brown eyes bathed in altar light, the image of an honest enterprise. He was buoyed by the attention and he seemed to be explaining the meaning of the sentences to the congregation, composed of many journalists. As he read I could hear an arc of intelligence:

> Think of the love that the Father has lavished on us, by letting us be called God's children; and that is what we are. Because the world refused to acknowledge Him, therefore it does not acknowledge us. My dear people, we are already the children of God, but what we are to be in the future has not yet been revealed; all we know is that when it is revealed we shall be like Him because we shall see Him as He really is.

'Wasn't the young lad great?' one of my colleagues said. I nodded and my shoulders relaxed a bit.

I had stayed up most of the previous night in our room in the Royal Marine, weighing my own words. Having been divorced from Bob, I was taking a risk, but who had known him better or mourned him more? After Communion it was my turn. Father Monahan called my name, smiled and gave me an encouraging nod. He adjusted the microphone for me and I began:

> On behalf of my son Conor, Bob's cousins in Cork and his family and friends in America, I'd like to thank you all for coming to St Michael's Church today.
>
> Thanks also to the many people who have supported us so kindly since we heard of Bob's untimely death at the age of fifty-six. Thank you for your sympathy.
>
> I am overwhelmed by the beauty of the service, the music and the homily by Father Monahan. It is helping me a great deal.
>
> I am grateful to my *Irish Times* colleagues, many of whom I see here today, who have been virtually an extended family to Bob and me since we came to this country in the mid-1980s, and to Norah Owens, who befriended and assisted Bob in the last years of his life.
>
> It is a comfort that Bob is being buried in Ireland. He loved this country. It is where his parents and his son were born. May he rest in peace here.

At that point a local woman wheeled a pram into the church, and pushed it all the way down the long centre aisle towards me. On and on she came, all the way to the front, seemingly oblivious to the fact that she was wandering around in the middle of a funeral.

For a moment I thought she was going to push the pram up on to the altar to join me. I stopped speaking, hoping that the silence might give the woman a clue. The baby let out a cry, a wisp of hope really, and the woman, realising where she was, rushed all the way back down the aisle and out of the church.

I continued with my eulogy:

> Now that Bob is gone, I want to remember him the way he was when I met him in 1980: tall, dark and handsome, gentlemanly, kind, intelligent, instantly likeable. I remember him in the newsroom of the *New York Daily News*: a lanky young reporter answering the phone in a baritone voice, almost singing the words, 'City Desk'.
>
> Despite the difficulties, and they were prolonged, gratitude remains. I am grateful to Bob for Conor.
>
> And to our son, I say: I know that you loved your father and I know that he loved you. Remember him and remember this day and take courage from it and from the people who came here. Love is stronger than death, Conor, and my gratitude to your father and my love for you will never die.
>
> Thank you.

I took off my reading glasses and folded my notes and began to walk slowly across the altar. The applause started softly and startled me at first, then grew and had a rippling effect, like waves of the sea. It was the gentlest, most supportive applause I have received, and at the most unexpected moment of my life. It helped me across the altar. As I passed Father Monahan, who was sitting in a chair, he smiled slightly and looked at me with compassion. You make friends in the strangest places, I thought; I had just made one for life on the altar. I walked slowly to my seat, past the Christmas camels and floral tributes, clutching my reading glasses and my piece of paper.

When the service ended, people formed a queue outside the church. They stood there so patiently on the cold but sunny January day. No one was restless and everyone seemed to know instinctively just what to do. Sympathy came from all corners of our lives. Face after face appeared before me. There was the poet Nuala Ní Dhomhnaill, whom Bob and I had taken out to lunch at Nodeldini's fish restaurant on the East Side when we lived in New York. She had written us a thank-you note from Ireland on black stationery with gold ink, and she and I had remained friends throughout the years. Darragh MacIntyre, Tom's son and now a journalist in his own right, shook Conor's hand. He had taken the train from Belfast to attend the funeral, Nuala said. Bob had hired him as a copy boy at the *News* shortly before we moved to Ireland.

Seeing Darragh reminded me of our move from New York on 22 July 1986, a day of jungle-like heat and humidity. We had quit our jobs and placed all our belongings on a ship headed for Cork. We flew to Shannon, drove to Cork city and arrived at a B&B. The woman of the house was annoyed at our arrival because she was watching Princess Diana's wedding, and the royal-watching in Cork mildly surprised me. Bob and I took a walk and I fingered the keys to my New York apartment, which were still in my handbag. We threw the key to the apartment into the River Lee.

Standing before me in the queue of mourners was Colonel E. D. Doyle, *Irish Times* contributor on military affairs for twenty years and the chief UN military observer in the Sinai Desert from 1975 to 1977. A renaissance man, Ned was a soldier, an electronics engineer, a writer and a military historian. Disciplined in every way, he was dapper and impeccably dressed. You could actually see yourself in his perfectly shined shoes, which were always ready for inspection, no matter which war had just broken out. We became friends during the first Gulf War in 1991 when I was expecting Conor. I would be working on the foreign desk when Colonel Doyle arrived in the *Irish Times* newsroom with his copy for the next day's paper. He had dealt with people from all over the world and I welcomed his internationalism. I often wrote the headlines and introductions to his pieces and adjusted small points of style. He used to refer to specific ships as 'she'; I couldn't allow him to do so because in *Irish Times* style a ship was referred to as 'it'.

'Could you hear what I said?' I asked him as he stood outside the church. I wondered how well the microphone had worked.

Ned, in his eighties, looked sorrowfully at Conor and me. 'Indeed I did.'

The sky was blue and the sea was calm as we stood in Shanganagh Cemetery. As the coffin was taken from the hearse, Conor said, 'Look, Mum.'

I held his hand tightly as we approached the grave.

'Stay close to the priest, Conor.'

Father Monahan was standing calmly at the edge of the grave, wearing his black leather jacket. The undertaker approached us with a microphone.

'No, no, no,' the priest and I said, shooing him away.

Father Monahan prayed. The coffin was hoisted and lowered into the grave, where it came to rest somewhat crookedly on the earth.

'Will they fix it?' Conor asked.

'I'm sure they'll straighten it later.'

But I wasn't absolutely sure.

Conor and I stood peering down at the coffin with its small brass plaque. We leaned over the edge of the grave, with Joan and her son Nicky wobbling beside us in the soft earth. The prayers ended, the mourners began to disperse and walk back to their cars or stop to talk in small groups, and as they did I paused for a moment and prayed that the men who filled in the grave would take the trouble to straighten Bob's coffin.

2

TALKIN' TO BRESLIN

'Mr Breslin?'

He did not look up.

I walked into his office. It was a small, bright, modern cubicle on the seventh floor of the *New York Daily News*'s art deco building on East 42nd Street between Second and Third Avenues in Manhattan. It was a Saturday in September 1979: there was no receptionist, no editorial assistant, no interference.

I stood in front of his desk.

He still did not look up. He said, 'I don't know any Mr Breslin.' He was typing on a heavy, old-fashioned, manual typewriter with big keys, and he kept typing. He used thick yellow copy paper which reproduced his column in triplicate.

I sat down in a chair opposite him and remained silent.

He was a large, rumpled fifty-year-old man with a mop of black hair going grey, a wrestler's middle and dark, thoughtful eyes that conveyed intelligence, warmth and a lot of pain. He was concentrating very hard and I did not speak; I didn't dare. I just sat there, looking out the window overlooking 42nd Street, waiting and thinking. I hadn't read much of his work growing up and I was thinking that I had some catching up to do.

After a while he said, 'Where are you from?'

'Chelsea, Massachusetts.'

'I know Chelsea.'

'How do you know Chelsea?'

'I know all places like that.'

I smiled and said nothing.

'Whaddaya want?' he asked, glancing up at me now. I was twenty-three.

'I'd like to follow you around on assignment,' I began. 'I have to write a profile for Columbia.' I paused. I didn't call him 'Mr Breslin' again, and he was too famous to call 'Jimmy' so I refrained from calling him anything. I waited.

He said nothing and went back to his typewriter. Occasionally he'd rip a page of copy from the carriage and throw it into the waste-paper basket.

I listened to the tapping of the keys and wondered what he was writing for tomorrow's paper.

Eventually he stopped. Slowly and methodically, he reached for a pen and a small piece of paper. In big, curly, almost childish handwriting he wrote down something on the piece of paper and handed it to me.

He had written down his name, his address in Forest Hills, Queens, and his home telephone number.

I looked at him in amazement and murmured, 'Thank you.' I continued to sit absolutely still. I thought he might want to eject an unexpected visitor from his office while he was trying to write his column, and he would be perfectly justified in doing so. But he just kept working while I watched and listened. Perhaps it was my silence that won him over. Finally he looked up from his desk and, to my even greater astonishment, he winked at me.

A few days later I met Barbara Belford, a former reporter for the *New York Herald Tribune* and my thesis adviser at Columbia, and told her, 'I've found my profile subject. I don't need to talk to anybody else.' During the next nine months, I followed Jimmy Breslin on assignment, meeting him at the Bronx Courthouse or at a federal building in lower Manhattan or in a restaurant in Queens, wherever the story took him. I learned to say as little as possible. 'I don't like to say too much in these places,' he said once. I didn't have to be told twice.

Sometimes people would ask him for his autograph and he would stop walking and sign. He was quiet; he was always writing in his head. He introduced me to his friends and cronies in Queens, Manhattan, Brooklyn and the Bronx as 'Miss Sullivan of Columbia University'. When he felt free to talk he asked me about Ireland and what I had done during my year there and who I had met and what writers I liked to read.

He was the best reporter I have seen in action and the best writer against a deadline. He didn't drive, so he took taxis or the subway or got lifts from other people. He also walked a lot, always looking around him and having conversations with people until he got what he needed. His eye for significant detail, his detachment from the media pack, his sympathy for the poor, his love of writing and his hard work put him at the top of the heap in the tough world of New York journalism.

I became a regular reader and admirer of his *Daily News* column, which he wrote three times a week.

At the time I was living at 5 East 51st Street, a five-storey, redbrick, rent-controlled building between Fifth and Madison Avenues, across the street from St Patrick's Cathedral and next door to Olympic Towers.

Apartment 5C, on the fifth floor, was my home for many years. The apartment consisted of one big room which doubled as living room and bedroom, an L-shaped hallway, a tiny kitchen and a bathroom that had seen better days. The living room window looked out on to the spires of St Patrick's. The bathroom window opened on to an air shaft, from which you could hear a singer practising her scales: 'La la la laaahh (pause) la la lah.' It looked like Paris from the living room and Italy from the bathroom. It was my haven in the big city, protected by the splendid cathedral with its stained-glass windows by artists from Chartres to Boston.

Andrew P. Quigley, *Chelsea Record* publisher and friend of my parents, held the lease on that apartment. My mother asked him to let me live there while I went to Columbia. The rent was one hundred and sixty-five dollars a month. When I moved in I told the building superintendent that I'd be there for three or four weeks; I stayed for seven years.

You never knew who you'd run into on East 51st Street. On my days off I would emerge from the building in jeans and a T-shirt, carrying a bag of laundry to the laundromat over on First Avenue. I would find myself in a sea of fancy people on their way to work. Once I stepped on to the sidewalk and swung the bag over my shoulder, just missing Alistair Cooke.

One morning, after waking up, I happened to look out the window and down to East 51st Street below. Crowds of people were watching a figure dressed in white who was walking slowly along the side of the cathedral. The crowds were shouting words I could not hear. I opened the window a crack. They were shouting, '*Viva Papa, Viva Papa.*' I took a closer look at the figure in white: it was Pope John Paul II, on a pilgrimage to St Patrick's.

Around this time I got a phone call from Jimmy Breslin that went something like this: 'Whaddaya doin' tonight?'

'Working at *Newsweek*.' I was doing minor research work for Dick Schaap, who was writing a book about Ted Kennedy. I would assemble facts on file cards in an office at the *Newsweek* building, which was located around the corner from my apartment.

'There's somebody I want you to meet.'

'Who?'

'Bernadette Devlin.'

I arranged to do the research for Schaap another night. Within an hour or two I was sitting in a bar on Second Avenue with Pete Hamill, Breslin and Bernadette Devlin McAliskey. 'Where's your notebook?' Pete Hamill growled at me. 'Everybody knows why you're here.'

I maintained my *omerta*-like silence in Breslin's company but managed to ask Bernadette what she thought of the recent visit of the Pope to New York.

'A spectacle for the deaf,' she said.

Apartment 5C had been uninhabited for some time and there was work to be done. My friend from the Fanad peninsula in Donegal, Joe McGee, who had arrived in New York in the late 1960s with a student visa and a desire to get out of the wind and the rain, helped me sand the floors and coat them with polyurethane. We painted the walls and got rid of the junk. It was modest work on a postgraduate student's budget, but we made the apartment habitable and clean.

I placed my electric typewriter on a folding card table in the L-shaped hallway and I wrote and wrote. I rented a piano. I looked at the spires of the cathedral. I walked over to Second Avenue to buy groceries and do my laundry. And that first summer, until I bought an air conditioner at Macy's and lugged it home in a taxicab, begging the cabbie to carry it up in the lift, I sat very, very still on the bottom of my bed in the suffocating New York heat.

Joe, who had the dark hair and eyes of Donegal, was from the village of Ballyheerin. A painter and a peripatetic reader of books, he gave me two apartment-warming gifts which I have to this day. One was a painting he did of Sean O'Casey as an old man, wearing a rich, reddish-burgundy throw and matching reddish-burgundy cap with white stars. In the painting, which is based on a photograph, O'Casey's eyes are closed and he appears to have nodded off to sleep while reading. His hand position suggests that he has dropped a book. Joe went to the Frick Museum and studied the use of light by Vermeer in order to do that painting. He gave me the artwork before the paint had dried.

His other gift was *A Treasury of Great Reporting: 'Literature Under Pressure' from the Sixteenth Century to Our Own Time*, a book I could reach for whenever I was, as he put it, 'fraught with journalistic fervour'.

The nine months at Columbia raced by in a fury of reporting, writing and editing assignments. The teachers were exciting, many of them top professionals. Film reviewer Judith Crist, a household name in America, selected me for her writing class. From 1965 to 1987 she was the movie critic for the weekly *TV Guide*, which, at its peak in the 1970s, had a circulation of seventeen million and an estimated readership of fifty million. She was exacting, generous with her energy, witty and occasionally caustic. Crist's criticism could send you diving for cover, but her praise made you sit up straighter and work harder at becoming a writer.

Irvin Horowitz, a *New York Times* editor for more than thirty years, was my news editing professor at Columbia. While working as assistant national editor, he co-ordinated the paper's daily assignments from early morning through the first-edition deadline. When he died in 1994 his obituary noted: 'For correspondents and freelance writers around the country, his gruff voice at the end of the telephone was often the voice of *The Times*.' Horowitz enjoyed recreating the busy atmosphere of an imaginary newsroom while we edited copy in his classes, held at night in the journalism building at 116th Street and Broadway. He talked at the top of his voice about his own working life to try to distract us while we were editing on deadline. Our very first assignment involved trying to write a headline on a poorly written and terribly convoluted story about a young man who had died in a domestic accident. The purple prose went on and on, and our job was to interpret the bad copy and summarise it in a four-word headline.

'Miss Sullivan is the only one who got the headline,' Horowitz roared at the end of class. 'LIFEGUARD DROWNS IN BATHTUB. Miss Sullivan, you're going to be a very fine editor.'

At the time I wanted to be a newspaper reporter or magazine writer. When the programme at Columbia ended, I packed my master's degree in my suitcase, locked the door of 5 East 51st Street, Apartment 5C, and went home to my parents. I had nothing lined up in Boston; it was purely a reflex action.

I hadn't talked to Jimmy Breslin in a while, for two reasons:

one, my profile of him was finished; and two, nobody's perfect and sometimes he was too gruff even for me. But less than a month after I left New York, I dialled his number in Queens and his wife Rosemary answered.

'Sheila, where've you been? He missed you.'

Breslin got on the phone. 'I think you ought to come down.'

At first I didn't understand what he meant. Come to New York? For what?

He said the *Daily News* was introducing an afternoon edition of the newspaper called *Tonight* and they were looking for reporters.

I was being thrown in at the deep end and the offer put me in a tight spot. New York was two hundred miles away and the break from my family would be wrenching; I was afraid it might be permanent. But I had just spent a year in Manhattan and the Boston journalism scene held little interest for me. I got into bed in Chelsea, pulled the quilts over my head and thought it over. How many chances like this came along in life? I needed a job and I wanted to work for a newspaper.

I bought a tan interview suit in Boston and took the train to New York to meet *Daily News* editor Mike O'Neill. It was extremely hot in New York that day and I was trying not to perspire too much and ruin my suit. O'Neill was a big, white-haired, gregarious man who laughed out loud when he saw me. His laughter, though not unkind, disconcerted me. The humidity wilted me.

After the interview, which was not too taxing, I stopped by to see Breslin in his cubicle. As usual, he was writing.

I told him what happened. 'Why do you think the editor laughed when he saw me?' I asked Breslin.

'So Irish.'

'Who – him or me?'

Breslin didn't answer. He kept typing. The next day, his column contained a cameo appearance by a young 'man' wearing a new tan interview suit. The young 'man' was nervous about looking for a job and was trying not to sweat too much.

I was hired.

I moved back into 5 East 51st Street, Apartment 5C, and I hit the ground running. On my third day as a reporter for the *Daily News*, in July 1980, I was working in police headquarters at 1 Police Plaza in Manhattan, across the street from City Hall. The reporters called the paper's police bureau 'the shack'. A call came in that a woman had been murdered at the Metropolitan Opera House. The victim was a beautiful, blond-haired violinist named Helen Hagnes Mintiks. The police bureau chief of the *Daily News* assigned me to the story.

'Where's the Met?' I asked.

I covered the story for days and weeks and spent a lot of time at Lincoln Center. Upset by the gruesome nature of the crime, I had nightmares about it for a couple of days. Back in the office, things were less sombre. They were trying to see if the headline 'Phantom of the Opera' would fit; it didn't. They settled on 'Murder at the Met'.

I phoned the poor woman's parents and got an interview with them and I talked to her bereaved husband, who was a sculptor. I was so new at the paper that the *Daily News* photographer took my picture at the scene with onlookers, not knowing that I was the reporter for the *News*. I just kept dialling phone numbers and asking people questions. It was my first experience of intruding on other people's grief to make a living.

'No blondes approached me yesterday,' I dictated to the rewrite man, quoting the conductor of the orchestra, who had appeared at a press conference about the search for the violinist's killer.

'No blondes approached me yesterday, either,' the rewrite man retorted in a Groucho Marx voice.

I kept dictating information taken down in a spiral notebook. The paper wanted any snippet of news. The police spokesman said Helen Hagnes Mintiks's shoes had been found on the roof of the opera house; I told that to the rewrite man. Earlier that week we had reported that her body had been recovered from the air shaft. For the next edition of the *Daily News Tonight* edition the rewrite man produced the immortal line: 'Her shoes were on the roof and her body was in the air shaft.'

A stagehand at the Met was convicted of her murder.

It was a far cry from my undergraduate years at Williams College and my term paper for Religion 101 on 'man's ontological obsession'. My *American Heritage Dictionary* defined ontology as 'the branch of philosophy that deals with being'. In fact, most of the people in my *Daily News* stories didn't have ontological obsessions because they were already dead: slashed or shot or stabbed or, in one case, struck by a loose cable on the Brooklyn Bridge.

I remember running across that fabulous bridge in 1981 with a *News* photographer, with the press pass around my neck flying in the breeze. A cable had snapped, killing a Japanese photographer, and the bridge had been closed to all traffic.

'What caused the cable to snap?' Sam Roberts, city editor of the *Daily News*, asked when I phoned the desk.

I had just interviewed a city engineer on the bridge and my answer was ready. 'Well, pigeon shit,' I said. 'The pigeon shit, when mixed with rain, formed an acid that caused the cable to corrode.'

'Call it pigeon droppings,' Sam said, and hung up.

I rushed everywhere in those days, pen and notebook in hand, press credentials around my neck on a chain, taking down quotes, interviewing witnesses, phoning police spokesmen, estimating crowds, describing scenes, explaining what happened and phoning the rewrite desk or racing back to the office to write my story.

Daily News stories weren't that long, so I developed an ear for a quote or a detail that would tell the story in a hurry. I had to compress.

I loved the life. People in the newsroom had a sense of fun despite the macabre content of some of our stories. The *Daily News* had good editors, copy editors, reporters and columnists in the early 1980s, many of whom now work at *The New York Times*, and there was a lot to learn from them.

However, I did not love covering crime scenes in this pre-Giuliani, pre-zero tolerance, crack cocaine era in New York City. In those days reporters still went to the scene; once people had drugs to protect it simply became too dangerous to go to some neighbourhoods.

On one occasion police in Brooklyn reportedly shot dead two young black men and injured another who, community activists claimed, were unarmed. I went to the scene. By this time I had a car with New York press plates, which allowed me to park in specified zones around the city.

'It was a shootout,' I was told by a young spokesman for the black community, 'but only one side had guns.' I wrote down the quote and dictated it to the rewrite man when I got to a phone.

As I was speaking to the spokesman for the black community in Brooklyn, Breslin showed up with one of his sons, who had driven him to the scene. 'You got your car?' he asked protectively. I nodded. He and his son left and went to the hospital, where he found the injured man's mother praying beside his hospital bed. Because I was doing the hard news story on the fatal shootings, he wrote his column about the mother of the injured young man. Finding a significant, unusual angle was exactly the way he worked.

The quote: 'It was a shootout but only one side had guns,' appeared in the newspaper the next day. When I repeated the line to Tom MacIntyre the next time he visited New York, he said, 'That's American poetry.'

In a city that big there was always something happening. At one point there was a madman running around the subway wielding a machete. You wondered sometimes: when is the man with the machete going to get me? A New York press pass didn't make you invulnerable, although sometimes I pretended that it did.

One time I was in the emergency room of a hospital, checking on the condition of a victim of the East Side Slasher, a deranged man who was going around New York stabbing people, sometimes fatally. 'What's a nice girl like you doing in a place like this?' a photographer asked. The question came to my lips several times that year.

You didn't have to go into bad neighbourhoods in New York to find yourself imperilled, either. One day on assignment I met a bishop, an old hand in the hierarchy, a pleasant person, not particularly cerebral. I wrote a naïve little article about something to do with the Catholic Church, and the bishop sent me a note of thanks. I was delighted to receive a letter from a bishop. I can still see the bishop's seal on the stationery. We kept in touch. I sent him a Christmas card; he sent me a note. I was friends with a bishop. That's New York, I thought. That's the newspaper world.

Then one day I bumped into the bishop outside St Patrick's Cathedral, around the corner from my apartment. He had been doing some business at the cardinal's residence. I was twenty-four, single and going out to meet a friend. It was a beautiful, sunny evening and I greeted the bishop warmly. We stood on the street corner. During the course of a brief conversation the bishop said he had been on my street, East 51st Street, recently and, as he had passed the doorway of my building, he had almost pressed the doorbell. I think his exact words were: 'I passed your building the other day. I almost rang the doorbell.'

I have gone over this event in my mind many times over the past twenty-five years, and yes, to the best of my recollection, his words were: 'I passed your building the other day. I almost rang the doorbell.' I am certain I heard the word doorbell.

I looked at the bishop. I couldn't comprehend it. I said nothing. You almost rang the doorbell? Of my tiny, modestly-furnished apartment? Why did you want to do that? I thought.

The bishop waited for a reaction. I may have said, 'Oh,' in shock, but definitely nothing else. I think he registered my dismay. I felt queasy but said nothing. I cannot remember how the encounter ended but I know that I was uncomfortable. I was not so sophisticated as to be able to handle calmly the thought of entertaining a bishop in my small apartment.

How green was my ally, one of my colleagues used to say. What I didn't know in 1981 would fill a very big book.

Did I challenge the bishop on it? No, I did not. I exchanged Christmas cards with him for another ten years.

Why? Like so many others, I had been brought up in a climate of automatic deference to the clergy. As a child, I saw my father stop in Logan Airport to kiss the ring of Cardinal Humberto Madeiros, Archbishop of Boston. The image was indelible. My father had bowed his head and kissed the archbishop's ring.

It took me a long time to tell Breslin the story, months stretching into years. Finally I mentioned it to him. As usual, he was way ahead of me on this one.

'Give me those letters from the bishop,' he roared over the telephone.

'No,' I said. I knew he would use them in a column.

'Give me those letters,' Breslin howled. 'Where are they?' he yelled. 'I want the letters from the bishop.'

'No.'

'How many letters were there?' He had an effective way of extracting information from me.

'Three, I think. They were short notes, not letters, and they were spread out over a few years.'

'And what did they say?'

'Well, they were friendly, though one or two were odd. When I told him I was getting married, he wrote me a note advising me not to use contraception.' The memory of it made me bristle.

'Give me those letters!' Breslin roared.

But I refused. I never gave him those letters.

When Bob and I moved to Ireland it was neither fashionable nor profitable. Unemployment and emigration were high and taxes were punitive. Jimmy Breslin did not think moving to Ireland was the brightest idea I'd ever had and he muttered darkly about us 'sitting in the rain with our one-way ticket stubs'. His opinion softened when I was hired by *The Irish Times* in the summer of 1987. He thought it was 'a lovely paper'. I had sent in my CV, been called to interview and been hired as a sub-editor. A senior editor told me he had phoned New York to check my references and had been told, 'She's one of the best reporters I've worked with.' He wouldn't tell me who said that, which I found odd, since I had no one to thank. Was it Breslin? Who knows? I never asked him.

The staff job which had been advertised was sub-editor, not reporter, so I had to shift my focus, learn a desk job and ask questions about the paper's then highly specific and formal house style. And I had to adjust to the conditions. Far from the high-tech world of New York, the newsroom in D'Olier Street resembled a Boston newspaper from the 1930s, with manual typewriters everywhere and phone lines hanging from the ceiling. We worked on 'hard copy' in those days, which means on paper instead of on computer screens, writing headlines with a pencil. 'That's fantastic,' Breslin said. The content of the paper intrigued me: comment, analysis and reaction to world events, rather than an emphasis on breaking news. In 1987 news didn't break in Ireland, except in the North; it seeped out. At first I found our reporting of domestic stories confusing. Sometimes one side of a story was presented one day and the opposing side was presented the next day; there was not always an attempt to get both sides of the story on the same day before the deadline. It was an Irish version of a newspaper, I concluded, with an emphasis on storytelling, reflection, discussion and argument.

I was relieved to be out of the rat race of New York and to be living in a slower, richer, Irish literary culture which compelled me. The non-stop work ethic of New York hadn't allowed much time for anything else, and what little spare time I had was spent with Irish friends talking about Irish books. I used to wander up to an Irish bookshop on the West Side to see the latest titles from Ireland. I used to look around the small Manhattan apartment and wonder, if I did have a baby, where was it supposed to grow up: on top of the refrigerator?

But in my darker moments the move to Ireland felt like identity suicide. Being seconded from home news to the *Irish Times* foreign desk, where I sub-edited stories about America, particularly American politics and presidential election campaigns, saved me and provided a vital link with the United States and the life I had known there for thirty years. Working on the foreign desk was an education after the insularity of American journalism. I had the chance to read thoughtful articles from correspondents, some in the Arab world, whose perspectives were vastly different from the prevailing world-views in Washington and New York.

Many journalists accustomed to having a byline and a public profile regarded sub-editing as tedious, thankless, anonymous and deadening, but having been a reporter and having run around New York for many years, I thought that being paid to read, write, edit copy and learn every night at a literary newspaper was a welcome change. My sub-editing colleagues approached their work with respect, meticulousness and knowledge. Some were among the best writers at the paper, working on books at home in the morning before coming to work in the afternoon.

Breslin kept in touch by telephone, reaching me at the paper or at home every once in a while when he got in an Irish mood. Through thick and thin for the past twenty years I have been in Ireland, he has always known where I was and how I was, and for this reason he is one of the truest friends I have had, in addition to being one of the greatest newspapermen America has produced.

Ring ring.

I'd pick up. 'Hello?'

'Yeah, whaddaya want?' he'd say. I was always glad to hear his gravelly voice.

'Whaddaya mean, whaddaya want?' I'd reply. 'You called me.'

He was usually writing a column.

'What's the difference between an al-Qaeda suicide bomber and an IRA bomber?' he asked.

I thought for a moment.

'Allah.'

'Good,' Breslin said. He was typing.

I pictured him in the cosy office of his apartment on the west side of Manhattan.

Sometimes he called to discuss the Irish divorce referendum or the Northern peace process or any other big, breaking story of the day with an Irish angle that interested him.

Once he mentioned that he was writing a book about the paedophile priest scandal in the Catholic Church.

'You go get them, Jimmy,' I yelled into the phone. I meant the bishops and cardinals, many of them with Irish last names, who knowingly moved paedophile priests around to different parishes in Ireland and the US. Newspaper columnists on both sides of the Atlantic were wondering aloud whether it was an Irish disease. I told him that the *Irish Times* style on paedophile priests was 'clerical sex abuse' at the request of the embattled Irish hierarchy.

'I don't believe it,' he said.

His book, *The Church That Forgot Christ*, about the sexual abuse of children by priests and the obscene cover-up of that abuse, was published in 2004. It is a cry from the heart about Breslin's feelings of betrayal as a Catholic. When I saw the book's dust jacket, I gasped. A picture of St Patrick's Cathedral, my old and trusted neighbour, was on the cover of the book. The cathedral was now the symbol of a scandal-ridden church.

At the time of the book's publication Breslin himself was being tested as a Catholic. His daughter Rosemary had died of a rare blood disease, aged forty-seven. She was the third of six children born to Jimmy and his first wife, also called Rosemary, who died of cancer in 1981. On 15 June 2004, I received a sad message on my answering machine:

> Hello, Sheila. Breslin. My daughter Rosemary died at eleven o'clock yesterday morning. This is the first chance I got to make a call to you. I'm sorry for everything and I'd appreciate a prayer.
>
> There'll be a service Thursday here in New York but we won't even look for you. All right. Thank you very much. I wanted to tell you. Thanks.

Like many Catholics, in his grief he was forced to separate a faith he loves from what he calls 'a failed Church in Rome' and 'a fraud inhabiting great buildings'. At times of bereavement he relied on his faith, 'which always gave me feelings of indescribable beauty', and not on the institution of the Church, 'an all-male club that is many centuries old and believes prayers to God must be heard over the sound of women scrubbing the floor'.

In *The Church That Forgot Christ* he wrote:

> I know I must attack this Church that has let paedophiles flourish, the victims to suffer for decades. But my upbringing in this Church that started at age four is not shucked off so simply, no matter what great hill of dark facts you gather. Your past prolongs indecision.

His daughter Rosemary's memorial service was held in the Church of St Francis of Assisi on West 41st Street. It was the church of Father Mychal Judge, the former New York City Fire Department chaplain and the first official victim of the

September 11 attack on the World Trade Center in 2001. I flew from Shannon to JFK to attend the service. The day was so hot and humid that, as I stood on West 41st Street, I swore I would never complain about Irish weather again. Then, mercifully, it began to rain.

'It reminds me of Ireland,' I said to *Daily News* columnist Michael Daly, a close friend of the Breslins.

'You're like an Eskimo in snow,' he replied kindly.

The church, as big as a cathedral, was filled with mourners and the biggest floral arrangements I have ever seen. Friends and neighbours from Queens and Manhattan mingled with journalists and writers, watched by Franciscan friars in brown robes. The church was so crowded there was room left for only two emotions: love and pain.

When all hope was gone, Rosemary had planned her own memorial service. She asked her brothers and sister to be funny and brief when they spoke, and they were. Her husband, Tony Dunne, spoke. And then it was the father's turn. Breslin is a writer who writes, and this tragedy was no exception. He walked slowly to the altar and gave the eulogy, 'A Daughter's Last Breaths'. He praised Rosemary's courage in bearing her illness and he evoked the memory of his first wife.

As he spoke I recalled Mrs Breslin, the former Rosemary Dattolico, who died three months after my father passed away in Boston. I remember visiting her in the hospital in New York. She was Italian-American, warm and cordial, with large brown eyes and a practical intelligence.

'Have you still got your apartment?' she asked me.

I nodded shyly, not wanting to tire her out with conversation. By that point I knew something about cancer and hospitals.

But Mrs Breslin chatted pleasantly while lying in the bed with a few months to live. She described her trip to California and the view of the Pacific Ocean. 'The waves, Sheila,' she said, waving her arm gently over her head. 'They went on for blocks.'

Jimmy is in his mid-seventies now and has stopped writing three times a week for *Newsday*, though his byline does appear once in a while. His final columns were seamless, as though written in a dream. Since then he has written a play, *Love Lasts on Myrtle Avenue*. He continues to write the way other people continue to breathe. He has mellowed over the years. He swims regularly in the pool in his apartment building and, far from the burly fellow I met in 1979, he is fit and slim. He is married to Ronnie Eldridge, former New York City Council member and true-blue New Yorker like he is. Robert Kennedy said of her: 'Behind that sweet motherly face Ronnie Eldridge has one of the toughest political minds in the city, if not the country.'

In 1994 Jimmy had surgery to remove an aneurysm from his brain. Following the successful operation he wrote *I Want to Thank My Brain for Remembering Me*, which, in my view, is his finest book. You can turn to any page at random and admire the writing. Consider the following offering in which Jimmy contemplates the role of Catholicism at times of personal crisis, the mystery of the sacrament of last rites and the journey of the soul of John F. Kennedy:

> There is no such thing as an ex-Catholic. At the start, you have no choice nor do you even know where you are or what they are doing. But once they put water on your head and an adult speaks for you, you are a Catholic for all the days through all the years until they pray over your grave.
>
> You can fall away from the religion as long as you please, for years, for decades; you can deny it through a thousand cock crows, you can luxuriate in sin. But let there be one sharp chest pain, one deep moment of dizziness, and that is some loud bawl that you let out for a priest.
>
> Perhaps the ambulance crew can save your life,

but for sure the priest saves your eternity.

The Catholic Church is held together by one word: calamity.

I'll tell you where I learned that best. Jacqueline Kennedy is in the waiting room outside of Emergency Room One, Parkland Hospital, where her husband was dead, and she was talking earnestly to the priest who had just given her husband the last rites of the Church. She nodded numbly and the priest touched her arm and left.

The priest's name was Oscar Hubner, and I found him that evening in the rectory of Holy Trinity Church, a handsome brick building in the Oaklawn area. It is about two and a half miles from the hospital.

'Mrs Kennedy asked me if this was a valid last rites,' he said quietly. 'I assured her that it was. The Church law is that there is about two hours from the time that death is pronounced and the soul departs from the body. If you administer the last rites during that period, it is a valid last sacrament. I anointed the president about an hour after he had been brought to the hospital. This was well within the two-hour period. I assured Mrs Kennedy of this and she said, "Thank you." She was relieved.'

I read a proof of that book sitting in Jimmy's apartment in New York. 'Though you may not have intended it when you started out as a sportswriter,' I told him, 'you have become a classic American memoirist.'

Once in a while I call him to tell him the news from Ireland.

Sometimes he phones me out of the blue and says in a low voice, 'Yeah, what about the letters from the bishop?'

'What about them?'

'I want them.'

I refuse.

He gets louder.

'Gimme those letters from the bishop.'

'No!'

'I want them!' he bellows and then he hangs up.

3

Happy Days in Killaloe

My father used to say that he was born at home on the kitchen table because he wanted to be close to his mother. The grandson of Irish immigrants from Cork, Frederick Joseph Sullivan was the son of a master plumber who built the pretty wooden house at 32 Willard Street in which my father, his sister Marie, and his brothers Vincent and John grew up in Chelsea, Massachusetts, the first city north of Boston across the Mystic River Bridge. The house on Willard Street had dozens of steps leading up to the front porch, from which you could see the air traffic at Logan Airport a mile or two away. I remember my grandfather, in his late eighties, sitting on that porch in spring and summer, watching the planes overhead come and go in the sky.

'What happened to the O in O'Sullivan?' I used to ask my father on the way home from visiting my grandparents.

'They dropped the O in the ocean.'

Having believed that he was born at home on the kitchen table, I had no reason to doubt this story either.

The O appears to have been lost in the Celtic mist but Irish placenames lingered in the folk memory. 'Happy days in Killaloe,' my grandfather would say when he raised a glass in toast.

'Happy days in Killaloe,' my father would reply.

My cousin, Karin Sullivan Killeen, is responsible for much of the scant information we have of our family's Irish origins on the dominant Sullivan side. My great-grandfather, Patrick Sullivan, was born in Cork in 1845 and emigrated from Ireland to Boston. My great-grandmother, Julia Fleming, was born in Cork in 1849. My father told me that she earned her passage to America by becoming an indentured servant to a family in Boston's Back Bay. Julia, aged fourteen, arrived in New York on 18 May 1863 on the ship *Harvest Queen* and married Patrick Sullivan in St Rose Church, Chelsea, Massachusetts, in the late 1870s.

The Boston my great-grandparents came to was a city in which newspapers ran ads for jobs which stated: 'Positively no Irish need apply.' Boston had been built on Yankee virtues imported by the *Mayflower* passengers who landed at Plymouth Rock in 1620. John Winthrop (1588–1649), governor of the Massachusetts Bay Colony, laid out his vision for a 'New' England when he told his Puritan colonists: 'For we must consider that we shall be as a City upon a Hill.'

In *The Boston Irish: A Political History*, Thomas H. O'Connor writes:

> The Irish had the misfortune of coming to a city that was already more than two hundred years old – positively ancient in terms of American cities – with a reputation that was awesome and a civic identity that was truly intimidating. The Yankee past, as William V. Shannon has observed, had produced the American Revolution, the Old North Church, Faneuil Hall, and Bunker Hill, along with families like the Otises, the Hancocks and the Adamses. And in more recent years the transcendentalist movement had turned out such incomparable literary talents as Emerson, Longfellow, Hawthorne and Thoreau.

Oliver Wendell Holmes (1809–94) – author, poet and professor of anatomy and physiology at Harvard, who was born in Cambridge, Massachusetts, and whose life spanned the nineteenth century

– called Boston's urban aristocrats 'Brahmins' after the priestly class of the ancient Hindus of India. O'Connor wrote that the Brahmins could be identified by the following distinctive characteristics: 'their houses by Bulfinch, their monopoly of Beacon Street, their ancestral portraits and Chinese porcelains, humanitarianism, Unitarian faith in the march of the mind, Yankee shrewdness and New England exclusivity'. They were hostile to the Irish immigrants, who were arriving in the United States in their droves as a result of the Great Hunger, and they abhorred the newcomers' Roman Catholicism.

My grandfather, Frederick Sullivan, was born in Chelsea in 1881. He married Matilda Hannabury, who was known as Helen, in St Rose Church, Chelsea, in 1911. Helen's grandparents had emigrated from Ireland to St John, New Brunswick, which in the mid-19th century was second only to Grosse Isle, Quebec, as the busiest port of entry for Irish immigrants to North America. Helen's parents were born in St John and she herself was born there in 1884, one of eleven children. The family name was changed from the Irish version, Henneberry, to Hannabury along the way.

My grandfather was a kind man, genteel and uncomplaining. The Depression of the 1930s affected his plumbing business and times could not have been easy as he and my grandmother raised four children. During the Second World War all three of their sons were drafted and their youngest, John, nicknamed Jack, was killed by a sniper in the Philippines on 9 May 1945, one day after the Allied victory in Europe was declared. I remember seeing Jack's Purple Heart medal in a drawer in the dining room in the house on Willard Street, along with a letter my grandparents received from the commanding officer of Company C, 632nd Tank Destroyer Battalion, informing them of the circumstances of his death so far from home. The letter, dated 13 June 1945, was addressed to my grandmother. It read in part:

Sergeant Sullivan was killed in action against the enemy on the afternoon of May 9, 1945 in the Cabaruan Hills near Malisiqui, Pangasinan Province, Luzon, Philippine Islands. At the time of his death he was a member of a combat foot patrol sent out on a mission of eliminating certain enemy resistance. In the performance of his mission, your son was killed by an enemy sniper. I assure you that his death came instantly and that he suffered no pain.

Sergeant Sullivan was buried in the United States Armed Forces Cemetery at Santa Barbara, Luzon, Philippine Islands, on May 10, 1945 with full Military Honors.

I was born in 1956 in Eisenhower's America, and by that time Irish-Americans in Massachusetts were making their way up the ladder, becoming a strong force in politics, trade unionism and the police and fire departments. Some attended university, obtained white-collar jobs in local, state and federal government, and began to penetrate the banking and corporate sectors. As a sub-culture within American culture, our crowning moment came in 1960 when John F. Kennedy, a proud Bostonian of Irish descent, was elected the country's first Catholic president.

Though tension remained between the Brahmins and the Irish – it tended to erupt in the editorial pages of the *Boston Globe* around St Patrick's Day – by the time I was growing up in the 1960s and 1970s, much of the power structure at local and state level was so Irish that it was hard to believe there was a time when we had not been in charge. My parents' lives and aspirations for their children, particularly in the area of education, reflected the improving circumstances and changing status of many, though not all, Irish-Americans.

My father was city auditor of Chelsea, which, in the 1970s, was an old, deteriorating but civic-minded city of 26,000 people living in an area of 1.8 square miles, a statistic often quoted in my youth. He was responsible for the city's finances and served as chairman of the Chelsea Retirement System for twenty-eight years. He was a trustee and member of the board of investment of the Atlantic Savings Bank and a trustee of the Soldiers' Home, a veterans' hospital in Chelsea. The city auditor's office was located upstairs in City Hall, a redbrick building with a gold dome and clock tower built in 1908 and designed by the Boston architectural firm of Peabody and Stearns to resemble a much smaller version of Philadelphia's Independence Hall.

He was six feet two 'in his stockinged feet', as he used to say. He was slim and handsome in a dark Irish way, with the hazel, watery eyes that you meet when you stroll down a street in Cork. He was rangy, like a baseball player, with a loose, long-legged walk that invited a song. Dapper but not vain, he wore white shirts with his initials monogrammed on the pocket and a felt hat with a feather in the brim, like Dana Andrews in *The Best Years of Our Lives*. I rarely saw him without a tie. He was the kind of man who carried a handkerchief and tipped his hat when he drove past a Catholic church. His manners were from another era and his preoccupations those of another world, one that was rapidly disappearing in the post-war America which he inhabited uneasily at times.

My mother, the former Mary Elizabeth Hanlon, worked in City Hall in Chelsea, too, one flight of stairs down from my father's office. She was administrative assistant to the superintendent of schools. She was five feet six and slim, with delicate features and auburn hair. The superintendent, J. Frank Herlihy, introduced my father to my mother one snowy afternoon in 1947 and suggested that the bachelor city auditor, aged thirty-three, give Mary, aged twenty-one, a lift home. They were married a year later. Thirty years and four children on from that lift home in the snow, my father and mother were both still working in City Hall.

My parents were New Deal-style Democrats, to whom voting and participating in the life of the small city were sacred duties. My mother, whose father died suddenly in 1936 when she was ten, worked for the school department for forty-eight years and became an institution within the city's institutions. Her political instincts were keen and she knew who was connected to whom and what mattered in local politics. She could be fierce but she had a strong sense of fairness and was always on the side of the underdog.

My mother was a democrat as well as a Democrat; she really believed that all people were created equal and that all deserved the same chances. She valued education and the opportunities it afforded above all else. All four of her children went to private secondary schools, graduated from university and earned master's degrees. My mother had a lot of drive and a wall of encyclopaedias and books to which I frequently referred. She expected a great deal from us. Her pride in her children's accomplishments was immense, matched only by my father's.

My parents presided over a household in which cultural pursuit and achievement were valued; it was a think-tank filled with books, newspapers, debate, music and artistic life, and it was hectic, too hectic sometimes, when all of us were around. Acquiring vast sums of money was not mentioned – nor was it seen as a particularly worthy ambition.

My brothers and sister all pursued interesting paths. The youngest, Frederick Jnr, became a resident actor with the Trinity Repertory Company in Providence, Rhode Island. He regularly performs Shakespeare and also teaches and directs. John, who studied animation at the Disney Institute, is a secondary school teacher on Cape Cod, where he teaches art and animation and presides over elaborate theatrical productions with enormous casts. Kathleen, the first-born, is a political science major, who, before she became a wife and mother of three, was the first woman budget director of the House Ways and Means Committee in the

Massachusetts legislature. She also served as deputy state auditor.

My mother loved to work and was innovative in her job. After the Vietnam War, when Cambodian refugees were entering Chelsea's primary school system in the 1970s, she put rice on the menu of the schools' hot lunch programme, thinking it might help the children in their adjustment to a new life in America.

My elegant, war-weary father, who was generally regarded as more reserved, less practical and less ambitious than my mother, had a touch of the poet and the acute sense of the absurd that comes from the same deep well as sadness. He was very well liked. He loved to read and listen to music. Born in 1914, he attended Boston College High School on scholarship, where he was taught Greek and Latin by the Jesuits. He attended Northeastern University School of Law but did not finish, saying he was discouraged by a glut of lawyers on the market. By the time I was born, he had been appointed city auditor.

He drove us to school in his Ford Country Squire station wagon with real wood on the sides and then gently made his way to City Hall at 500 Broadway. He returned from work at 4.20 every afternoon, parked the car on the street below and, just as gently, made the long climb up the steps to the wooden house at 41 Jefferson Avenue, painted green with white diamonds on the porch. Then he would settle down to read.

My strongest memory of my father is the absorption with which he read. There was always a pile of books, magazines and newspapers beside his armchair in the living room. He'd begin with the *Chelsea Record* to get all the local news. The paper was owned and published by his friend Andrew Quigley, who wrote large sections himself. My father used to say that Andrew, who had many of the gifts of a nineteenth-century Irish orator, had memorised Bartlett's *Familiar Quotations*. If you knew Andrew or were a regular reader of his 'Off the Cuff' column in the *Chelsea Record,* that claim was difficult to dispute. Once, in an editorial opposing a strike by local schoolteachers in Chelsea, Andrew invoked Cicero: 'The gates of the city are open – depart at once.' He was in no doubt about the seriousness of the situation. 'We stand at Armageddon,' he wrote, warning his readers of the impending confrontation between the school committee and the teachers.

After he finished reading the *Chelsea Record*, my father would pick up the *Boston Globe* and turn to George Frazier, its lyrical and provocative columnist. Frazier wrote four times a week for the paper and once, when asked by an interviewer which came first, friendship or work, he replied: 'That's phrasing it a little harshly,' adding: 'I make no bones about it. I'm a lonely man. The column precludes friendships.'

Frazier, from an Irish-American family in South Boston, attended Boston Latin School, America's oldest public school. He graduated in 1928 and forever after he referred to Latin as his 'native tongue'. He was also an ardent Red Sox fan. One day in April 1973 when I was sixteen, my father held up a copy of the *Globe*. On the front page was an article by Frazier written entirely in Latin. The headline was 'Tibialibus Rubris XV, Eboracum Novum V'. Translation: 'Red Sox 15, New York 5'. It was his account of a game at Fenway.

Frazier was a member of the class of 1932 at Harvard, where he won the Bowdoin Prize for excellence in writing. As an undergraduate he sent three unsolicited manuscripts to *Vanity Fair* magazine, which published all of them. In his columns he often wrote about the 'lost generation' of American writers who had gone to live in France in the 1920s. He sparked my interest in the novels of F. Scott Fitzgerald, particularly *The Great Gatsby*, and other expatriate writers, such as Gertrude Stein, who wrote the strange and brilliant memoir *The Autobiography of Alice B. Toklas*. I loved *Gatsby* as much as Frazier did and I knew its opening lines by heart:

In my younger and more vulnerable years my father gave me some advice that I've been turning over in my mind ever since. 'Whenever you feel like criticizing any one,' he told me, 'just remember that all the people in this world haven't had the advantages that you've had.'

Frazier was one of America's first published jazz critics and he wrote well about jazz, especially Billie Holiday. He wrote columns about Nantucket Island, which he visited in September, and about Manhattan, where he loved to stay at any time of year.

He was a Bostonian who preferred New York, which reportedly created some tension with his *Globe* editors, and he kept an apartment on West 83rd Street for many years. 'Boston's great,' he wrote, 'but New York's the varsity, baby.'

One of his hang-outs was Tim Costello's bar in New York, which had James Thurber murals on the walls. In a column in October 1973, Frazier saluted the saloon-keeper, who had died, and his legendary watering hole, which faced the wrecker's ball:

> This country, at least in our time, has never known a literary saloon the like of Tim Costello's, and now it is to be no more, a sacrifice to a skyscraper, a victim of the high-rise culture that divests a city of its small graces; its proud heritage. Without Himself, who has been in the ground and as one with the heather on the heath these many unstylish years, Tim's was never as it was when he was there softly singing 'John Anderson, my Jo', discussing the Dublin of Joyce with Gogarty, or coming to the editorial aid of some *New Yorker* writer who sought his counsel about the turn of a phrase, the choice of a word.

Tim Costello was singing a love song by Robert Burns (1759–96):

> John Anderson, my jo,* John,
> When we were first acquent,
> Your locks were like the raven,
> Your bonnie brow was brent;*
> But now your brow is beld,* John,
> Your locks are like the snow;
> But blessings on your frosty pow,*
> John Anderson, my jo!
>
> John Anderson, my jo, John,
> We clamb the hill thegither;
> And monie a canty* day, John,
> We've had wi' ane anither:
> Now we maun totter down, John,
> But hand in hand we'll go,
> And sleep thegither at the foot,
> John Anderson, my jo.

Gloss
jo: sweetheart
brent: smooth, unwrinkled
beld: bald
pow: pate
canty: cheerful

Frazier's columns transported us to another world and demonstrated the power of language to transform an ordinary afternoon. Watching my father read him and then reading him myself was the beginning of my relationship with newspapers.

Apart from reading, my father's favourite pastime was listening to classical music, and he regarded concert pianists with something approaching awe. He thought playing the piano was a higher calling, and I inherited that reverence from him. Often after dinner, he'd reach for a Marlboro and ask me to turn on the record player. He'd want to hear Rachmaninov's *Piano Concerto No 2 in C minor* played by Vladimir Horowitz. Born in Kiev, Horowitz had married the daughter of conductor Arturo Toscanini and settled in the United States. When the concerto was finished my father would listen to *Rhapsody on a Theme of Paganini*. The music permeated the house on so many evenings that the works of Rachmaninov came to be engraved on my heart.

My father regretted not being able to play the piano so much that he and my mother ensured that I could. I took lessons from an early age, five or six, when my feet could not even reach the pedals. First I went to the local Catholic school, St Rose, for lessons. I recall a nun in full habit with a pointer, tapping on my tiny fingers when I hit the wrong key. I spent much of my childhood playing the piano at home, sitting under a framed poster of Toulouse-Lautrec's *Jane Avril*, a wedding present to my parents from Andrew Quigley.

Later, when my feet could reach the pedals, my father drove me across the Mystic River Bridge to Storrow Drive in Boston, past the Charles River and then to Brighton, to take private lessons at Mount St Joseph Academy, a Catholic secondary school for young women. The Mount, as it was known, was established in 1885 by the Sisters of St Joseph, a congregation founded in the seventeenth century in the French city of Le Puy, in response to a call from the Archbishop of Boston, John Joseph Williams. The Archbishop wanted to develop a Catholic school system for the growing immigrant population of the late nineteenth century.

Sister M. Olivia, born Irene Collins, a graduate of Smith College and the New England Conservatory of Music, was my piano teacher at the Mount for the next ten years. A small, saintly figure, she had been on her way to a career as a concert pianist when her father died and she entered the convent instead. Sister

Olivia had the simplicity of greatness; she had been a pupil of a pupil of Liszt and she instilled in me a love of classical music the like of which some children bring to religious faith. I grew up at the piano by her side, beneath a picture of St Cecilia, the patron saint of music. She talked about the difficulties of being a concert pianist, of needing a patron. It sounded like a lonely, difficult life, with long hours of practice. While I didn't want such a life, I believed that playing at that level was achievement of the highest order.

Her old rooms at the Mount each had two upright pianos. Every week I found her sitting quietly in the light coming through her window, looking as though she were posing for Vermeer. There was stillness, serenity and integrity of purpose in her music rooms, a link to the nineteenth century and the Romantic composers. She loved Liszt, Mendelssohn, Schubert and Schumann, but she loved Chopin most of all. She taught me his *Étude No 3 in E major*, subtitled *Tristesse* (Sadness). The étude, dedicated to Liszt, contains a melody so beautiful that Chopin said he never wrote another one to equal it. When one of his pupils played it to him at a lesson, Chopin said sadly: 'Oh, my homeland.' I also studied Liszt's *Étude de Concert No 3*, known as *Un Sospiro* ('plaintive sigh' in Italian), and Chopin's *Fantasie Impromptu*.

All works to be performed for an audience had to be memorised. Sister Olivia had a number of Steinway grand pianos on which she and her pupils gave annual recitals. The week before I graduated from the Mount, we held a small, private recital. I was heading off to college 150 miles away and ending my lessons; I was leaving her. We played Mendelssohn's *Scherzo, Opus 16, No 2* together in her modern, spacious rooms in the new convent, knowing that it would be the last time. She was at a baby grand; I was at an upright. Though she was in her eighties she could still play like lightning. My father was the person who clapped longest at the piano recital.

My father's life had been shaped by the Second World War and his experiences in wartime England, France and Germany marked him in ways that were impossible for me to understand. As a teenager it was difficult for me to imagine him, by then an older man reading in the living room, as he was during the war.

Photographs of him show a grinning young GI in uniform, healthy and trim, standing outside a castle in England or in a field in France. He had been a Morse code operator in the air force. In one small black-and-white photograph from the period he is standing behind a truck with his shirtsleeves rolled up, revealing strong muscles. 'That's when I had arms,' he said.

Like many veterans of that era he gave short answers to questions about the war.

'Did you ever fire a gun, Daddy?'

'Yes.'

'Did you ever kill anybody?'

'Not that I was aware of.'

'Who was your favourite general?'

'Omar Bradley.'

'What was your worst fear?'

'That the war was never going to end. That I was never coming home.'

He would pull down an atlas and turn to the map of Germany. His finger would find Aachen, where, just after the war ended, he had driven a jeep along a road filled with wraithlike prisoners released from the concentration camps. His passenger was an American colonel who had attended Williams College and who could speak fluent French. I grew up hearing about the Battle of the Bulge in the Ardennes, and the Blitz in London, both of which my father had experienced, and Hitler's 'Eagle's Nest' in Obersalzberg, near Berchtesgaden, Germany, which my father and other soldiers had been allowed to visit after the war.

Having been born on 6 June 1956, the twelfth anniversary of D-Day, I became interested in the Normandy landings, trying to imagine French beaches which were named after locations in the American midwest and west: Omaha Beach, Utah Beach.

After the war in Europe ended my father was still overseas when he received a letter informing him that his younger brother, Jack, had been killed in the Philippines. Over the years my father kept his grief to himself, but it ran deep. Many times I saw him turn to 'Last Poems, XVIII', in his blue hardback copy of A. E. Housman's *Complete Poems*. Again and again he would read Housman's lines:

> The rain, it streams on stone and hillock,
> The boot clings to the clay.
> Since all is done that's due and right
> Let's home; and now, my lad, good-night,
> For I must turn away.
>
> Good-night, my lad, for nought's eternal;
> No league of ours, for sure.
> To-morrow I shall miss you less,
> And ache of heart and heaviness
> Are things that time should cure.
>
> Over the hill the highway marches
> And what's beyond is wide.
> Oh soon enough will pine to nought
> Remembrance and the faithful thought
> That sits the grave beside.
>
> The skies, they are not always raining
> Nor grey the twelvemonth through;
> And I shall meet good days and mirth,
> And range the lovely lands of earth
> With friends no worse than you.

But oh, my man, the house is fallen
That none can build again;
My man, how full of joy and woe
Your mother bore you years ago
To-night to lie in the rain.

My paternal grandparents lived well into their nineties, dying peacefully of natural causes, but my father did not have so fortunate a fate. He died of bladder cancer in 1981, aged sixty-seven, when I was twenty-four.

The surgeon said: 'I'm sorry. You only get one daddy.' My sister and I were sitting with our mother in a well-lit room in a grey medical office building opposite St Elizabeth's Hospital on Cambridge Street in Brighton, down the street from the Mount. The doctor had come out from behind his desk and was standing before us, head tilted kindly to one side, hands in the pockets of his white coat. He had removed my father's bladder the previous morning. He was an alert, silver-haired, refined man of medium build and distinguished reputation who talked simply, the way highly intelligent people often do. He could not save my father from the black mass that had engulfed him. That's what he was telling us now.

We thanked the surgeon for everything he had done and left his office in silence. We stood outside the hospital and looked hard at the snow, which was piled high on both sides of the walkway. My sister and I huddled in our long, dark overcoats. My mother looked slight in her leather coat and fur-trimmed ankle boots, her features hidden under a silk scarf. There must have been three feet of snow on the ground, which was not unusual for Boston in winter, but with the shock of the news, the intense sunlight in our eyes and the glare on the drifts, the snow was difficult to absorb.

'He's going to die,' Kathy said.

'I know,' I replied.

It was November 1980. Within days I had sub-let my Manhattan apartment, begun an unpaid leave of absence from my job as a reporter for the *New York Daily News* and driven shakily from New York to Boston.

The finality of the surgeon's words prompted a near round-the-clock vigil which lasted through the final two months of 1980 and the first three months of 1981.

'How was he today?' my sister asked me one evening when she arrived at the hospital after work.

'Like a crazy little lamb,' I said.

My father was wearing his reading glasses and looking at the *Chelsea Record* when I first saw him that day. Things were eerily normal, despite the tube inserted down his throat. I kissed him on the forehead, took off my coat and sat in a bedside chair. After a while my father put down the newspaper, looked at my anxious face, gracefully waved a bony index finger in my direction, and said slowly and solemnly: 'I want you to go and tell the nurse to bring me the surrey with the fringe on top.' He was referring to a song in the Broadway musical *Oklahoma!* by Rodgers and Hammerstein. The medication was beginning to take effect.

Visitors came and went. The telephone rang. Relatives, friends and colleagues from City Hall, all swollen with grief. The cancer was relentless and he began to fade away.

Sometimes his mind was startlingly lucid. When someone kept him too long on the telephone, he'd say: 'Thank you for phoning. I've got to go now. The nurse is coming,' although the nurse was nowhere in sight. On it went over the difficult months: one day he'd be discussing Red Sox scores, the next day he'd sleep through my visit. Increasingly, when he was awake, it was as if he was watching imaginary television screens on the hospital wall, showing people and places from the sixty-seven years of his life. The lines between waking and sleeping, the present and the past, the living and the dead, were becoming blurred.

'Sssssshhhh,' he warned me one wintry February afternoon as

I sat by the side of the bed watching him. He put a finger to his parched lips to silence me. 'Do you hear that?'

'What is it, Daddy?'

'*Clair de lune*.'

I sat in the hospital room with my dying father, listening to the Debussy in his mind.

From time to time my father asked when he was going to leave the hospital and he became agitated and distressed when he didn't receive a reply. Kathy decided to tell him, in my presence, that he wouldn't be coming home. He looked away sharply for several moments while the large brown eyes in his gaunt face absorbed the news. He patted his chest once gently with his right hand and said, 'I don't fear death.' That night I stayed late at the hospital. At around 3 a.m. he suggested I go home, and, as I headed for the door of his hospital room, he said, '*Bonsoir.*'

'*Au revoir,*' I said, smiling at the ritual from my childhood.

'*Arrivederci.*'

'*Auf Wiedersehen.*'

'*Sayonara.*'

'*Adios.*'

'*Gute Nacht,*' he said.

'Goodnight, Daddy.'

After that the morphine did a lot of the talking. I sat by the bed with my memories. 'Where are you going, Daddy?' I used to call when he went out in the evening, to a trustees' meeting at the bank or the Soldiers' Home.

'Down to the city scales to get weighed,' he'd reply.

'Can I go, too?' I'd plead, as he quietly closed the front door.

During this period I dreamed he was in a huge, packed auditorium somewhere in Boston, lying on a stretcher. When he sat up, the audience applauded wildly; when he lay down on the stretcher, they groaned in despair. He sat up, then he lay down, with the audience applauding and groaning, until I woke up.

On the day of his funeral, a bright, crisp morning, the cortège drove once around City Hall in Chelsea before stopping in front of the fire station in Fay Square. We all looked out the windows of the black limousine to see why it had halted. And then we heard the bells. The firemen from the station, in blue dress uniform and white gloves, were lined up with their equipment. Andrew Quigley noted the next day in the *Chelsea Record:* 'As the hearse passed by, the firemen stood at attention and saluted, and the bells on the fire engine were tolled.'

A few months after he died, a box of letters my father had written during the war turned up, which showed an untapped literary talent. One, to his mother and my great-aunt Louise, written from Sioux Falls Army Technical School in South Dakota, dated 7 January 1942, reads:

> Dear Ma and Louise
> It takes me a little while to express it, but I am sure that you understand that my gratitude is not lessened by its tardiness. I speak, of course, of your can of cookies.

Another, written to his sister Marie from somewhere in Europe and dated 1 October 1944, was more wistful and despondent:

> Hello Marie
> As far as baseball is concerned I don't know a thing about the game any more. The daily scores are published in our army newspaper, but I have long ceased to care what place the team is in or who is pitching for whom. It all seems like part of another world that is now long ago and far away. It is just a memory, like an ice cream soda, or clean sheets, a blue necktie or a street lamp. You just have to forget about them until the world comes to its senses again. And maybe it won't be too long.

4

DISCOVERING IRELAND

Williams College is a small, private, liberal arts institution tucked away in the Berkshire Mountains of Massachusetts. With a brilliant faculty, a student body numbering about two thousand and an endowment of more than one billion dollars, it is one of America's finest and most privileged colleges. The campus, spread out along Route 2, the Mohawk Trail, in the north-western corner of the state, is about a three-hour drive from Boston. Psychologically it is an even greater distance away.

The college was founded with a bequest from Colonel Ephraim Williams of the Massachusetts militia, who was shot in the head and killed in 1755 at the Battle of Lake George while fighting French and Indian forces. He and his British and colonial troops were trying to drive the French from North America. The colonel left his bequest on condition that the town of West Hoosac be renamed Williamstown and that a free school be established there.

The trustees of that school petitioned the legislature to set up a tuition-based college. In 1793, seventeen years after the American Revolution and four years after the ratification of the US Constitution, Williams received its charter. It began as an all-male country college with a strong white Anglo-Saxon Protestant ethos and continued that way for almost two hundred years. In the early 1960s it phased out fraternities and in 1970 became co-educational. I was a member of the graduating class of 1978.

When I received my acceptance letter I thought, let's go

and see where they've been educating the men. I found a highly competitive academic environment in a quiet, pastoral setting, and I worked hard to keep up with the demands of the various courses. I read and I read and almost never let up. Once I spent an entire Thanksgiving break at home in my old bedroom on Jefferson Avenue in Chelsea reading *On the Groundwork of the Metaphysic of Morals* by Immanuel Kant, underlining important passages with a yellow marker.

'Do you have a warm coat?' was my father's only question as I was leaving to go back to the Berkshires.

It was an ideal world in which to read and write and think. In the autumn, tourists drove along the Mohawk Trail and craned their necks to see the New England foliage that had burst into a riot of colour; I called them 'the leaf people'. In the winter I walked to the Francine Clark Art Institute, filled with priceless artworks, and sat in front of Frederic Remington's *The Scout*. There was a great solitude in that museum in December, with the wind-chill factor below zero and the hills covered in snow. I studied the blues in Remington's study of the Native American, which is subtitled: *Friend or Foe?* In spring I trudged to classes through the mud; in early summer I sat on grassy banks and read.

Along with its faculty, its idyllic surroundings and its progressive views on co-education, Williams prided itself on its independence of spirit and quirky traditions. For example, the college's colour was purple. The reason? At the first Williams–Harvard baseball game in 1869 the players had no uniforms, and the spectators, who were watching the ball game from their carriages, had some difficulty in telling the teams apart. So Winston Churchill's mother went off to buy ribbons in a nearby millinery store to pin on Williams players, and the only available colour was the 'royal' purple. Wait a minute: Winston Churchill's mother? Yes, Jennie Jerome from Brooklyn, New York, who later became Lady Randolph Churchill, went off to buy the ribbons. What was she doing in Williamstown, Massachusetts? Her family summered there. Why was she at the Williams–Harvard baseball game? Possibly she was a baseball fan or knew someone on the team. Winston was born in 1874, five years after the purple ribbon-shopping episode.

During my freshman year I lived in Fayerweather Hall, an all-female dormitory. I wrote an article for the fledgling campus literary magazine about George Frazier, who had died on the day I graduated from the Mount. A young man who lived next door in the all-male dormitory came over to my room to discuss the piece. He had blue eyes, long black hair and a sensitive face. He sat on a chair in my room, smiled and was generally appreciative of the article. He smoked a cigarette and made a couple of changes to the copy, while I sat, fascinated by the editing process and by having a sophomore in my dorm room. His name was Jay McInerny. Years later when I was living in New York in the 1980s, a friend handed me a paperback novel: McInerny's *Bright Lights, Big City*. Written in a spare, ironic style, it became a defining work of my generation. I read it with delight at his cleverness, and pleasure at having known him slightly in college.

As someone who intended to major in English at Williams I soon became aware that many literary giants had left their mark on the Berkshires and the surrounding region: Herman Melville and Nathaniel Hawthorne in Pittsfield; Emily Dickinson in Amherst; Henry David Thoreau in Concord, and poet William Jennings Bryant in Williamstown. One of the first short trips I took was to visit Robert Frost's grave in Bennington, Vermont, which was about half an hour's drive. I stood over his gravestone and read his epitaph: 'I had a lover's quarrel with the world'.

Thoreau, poet, writer and transcendentalist, visited Williams in 1844, a year before he went to the woods to live deliberately near Walden Pond and ten years before *Walden* was published. He praised the college's location at the base of Mount Greylock, the highest point in the Commonwealth of Massachusetts, saying, 'It would be no small advantage if every college were thus located at the base of a mountain.'

Herman Melville lived at Arrowhead, a mustard-coloured farmhouse in Pittsfield, Massachusetts, from 1850 to 1863. Melville named the house after the artefacts he dug up while ploughing his fields. He wrote four novels, sixteen short stories and a volume of poetry during his years there. Of these works the greatest was *Moby-Dick*, his masterpiece about Captain Ahab aboard the *Pequod* and his monomaniacal hunt for the great white whale. Arguably the greatest American novel, it was published in 1851 and dedicated to Nathaniel Hawthorne. Melville wrote the novel at Arrowhead in his upstairs study facing north, where he was said to be inspired by Mount Greylock. From his window he could see the mountain, which reminded him of a rising sperm whale tilting its head out of the water slightly. Here he wrote one of the most famous opening paragraphs in American literature:

> Call me Ishmael. Some years ago – never mind how long precisely – having little or no money in my purse, and nothing particular to interest me on shore, I thought I would sail about a little and see the watery part of the world. It is a way I have of driving off the spleen, and regulating the circulation. Whenever I find myself growing grim about the mouth; whenever it is a damp, drizzly November in my soul; whenever I find myself involuntarily pausing before coffin warehouses, and bringing up the rear of every funeral I meet; and especially whenever my hypos get such an upper hand of me, that it requires a strong moral principle to prevent me from deliberately stepping into the street, and methodically knocking people's hats off – then, I account it high time to get to sea as soon as I can. This is my substitute for pistol and ball. With a philosophical flourish Cato throws himself upon his

sword; I quietly take to the ship. There is nothing
surprising in this. If they but knew it, almost all men
in their degree, some time or other, cherish very
nearly the same feelings towards the ocean with me.

Given the grandeur of the novel and the fact that I was living
near the mountain which inspired it, *Moby-Dick* dominated my
life for a while, particularly in my senior year. David Langston,
an assistant professor of English and son of a minister, taught the
book with intensity and zeal. He was a big, amiable man in his
thirties, with reddish-brown hair and a beard, who had grown up
in Oregon, Washington, Texas and Oklahoma. He had a PhD
from Stanford, which thrilled me because in 1977 I thought that
anyone from Stanford who drove a white Volkswagen Beetle with
a roof-rack and wore a leather jacket must be a radical. He talked
about structuralism and Lévi-Strauss and Marxism, and he taught
me new ways to analyse literature. He encouraged me to take my
views seriously and express ideas forcefully when necessary. David
made me think that you could have a wonderful life in a world
which revolved around books.

The college operated on the principle that students would
prosper in small classes where they would know their professors
well and receive individual attention. Many of my professors
did become my friends, among them James MacGregor Burns,
who won the Pulitzer Prize for his 1956 biography of FDR,
Roosevelt: The Lion and the Fox. He encouraged me to apply to
Columbia, America's most highly regarded postgraduate school
of journalism.

Don Gifford, a Joycean and long-time professor of English
affectionately known as 'Giff', sparked my interest in Irish literature. I remember Giff drawing the River Liffey on the blackboard
when we were reading *Dubliners*. In 1967, with the assistance of
Robert Seidman, Giff published *Notes for Joyce: An Encyclopaedic
Handbook of Facts and Allusions in* Dubliners *and* A Portrait of the

Artist as a Young Man. In the preface, he said he wrote the book because, when teaching *Portrait*, he found that he was spending most of his time in the classroom explaining the vocabulary and the allusions and too little time in direct discussion of the book itself. 'The result was not as much the process of teaching as it was a parade of erudition.' He died in May 2000.

During my junior year in 1977 I signed up for spring semester abroad in London, and visited Ireland for the first time. I lived in a run-down basement flat in a once-splendid building in Onslow Gardens and attended courses at the City of London Polytechnic. My professors were colourful and articulate and some had Irish connections. My art history professor was a descendant of General Michael Collins; she was a slender young woman named O'Brien-Twohig who carried an elaborate walking stick. A young male professor with shoulder-length hair and socialist politics asked me to write a paper on Anglo-Irish relations. He sent me to the library of the University of London, where I read the prison letters of Patrick Pearse.

In London I saw a Royal Shakespeare Company production of *Wild Oats* by Irish dramatist John O'Keeffe (1747–1833) and I went to see the play at least three times. I had never heard a speaking voice more beautiful than that of Alan Howard, who starred; nor had I ever seen a more immaculate stage production. The language of *Wild Oats*, which was electrifying, was my introduction to Hiberno-English.

In June 1977 I travelled from London to Holyhead by train and then to Dublin by boat. The crossing was rough. I met my parents, who had flown from Boston, and we drove around the west of Ireland. The informality was a relief after London. We visited Connemara: we found Alcock and Brown's landing site near Roundstone, County Galway, and saw the house in Rosmuc where Patrick Pearse went to learn Irish.

Three months later, back at Williams for my senior year, I saw a notice seeking applicants for a fellowship to the Watson

Foundation of Benefit Street in Providence, Rhode Island. The Thomas J. Watson Fellowship provided a grant for one year of independent study and travel abroad. I decided to apply to live in Ireland.

At precisely the time I was considering applying for a Watson, there was a 'swap' in the English Department. While I had been away in London, Giff had arranged an exchange with an Irish writer who had been living on an island off the west coast of Ireland. Giff was on Inishbofin, the island of the white cow, looking into lakes, drawing maps and investigating erosion caused by sheep. The Irish writer was living in Giff's house in Williamstown, preparing to teach at the college for one semester. The synchronicity was undeniable, although I wouldn't have called it that at the time.

Tom MacIntyre, from Bailieboro, County Cavan, a writer and former teacher at Clongowes, was then in his mid-forties. With his long white hair and beard, he had the air of a fisherman and he stood out on the Williams campus. His gaze could only be called perspicacious and his manner of speaking was best described by an English journalist as 'an oracular burr'. In conversation he used French, Latin, Irish and archaic English phrases mingled with American slang. I once heard him air the word 'winegall' to describe 'the slurpy, rainbowy thing in the sky'. His use of language as bits of music reminded me of *Wild Oats*.

'It's as if you just got off the boat,' he said at our first meeting, noting my surname and the obvious Cork ancestry. I knew that the rest of America regarded the Boston Irish as a sub-culture but I didn't know that the Irish Irish did too.

Tom's creative writing class was full but he allowed me to audit one of his lectures. 'I'd like to keep you around for entertainment value,' he said.

'Why do the Irish laugh so much?' he asked the students.

They sat in silence, pondering this cultural enigma.

I raised my hand. 'To keep from crying?'

He mentioned that his collection of short stories, *Dance the Dance*, had been published in 1970. I wrote to Faber and Faber in London and ordered a copy of the book. A few weeks later a small brown package containing a pink book with yellow, white and red letters on the cover arrived in my box in the college mailroom. At the time, ordering a book from England was, to me, an exotic enterprise. I read it with delight. The first story was 'Stallions', which Gus Martin of UCD had called 'a minor masterpiece'; others included 'Willy Wynne, *Con Moto*' and 'An Aspect of the Rising'.

I told Tom about my Watson proposal to live in Ireland for a year. He immediately suggested a topic – the study of nationalism in contemporary journalism and politics – and was generous with names of friends and contacts in the Irish arts world. I packed them into my tightly-knit proposal.

Tom hosted a small dinner party at Giff's house, attended by, among others, the chairman of the English department and his wife, another Irish-American student from Boston, and myself. At the dinner were two visitors from Ireland, Margaret and Miko Day of Day's Hotel, Inishbofin, County Galway. Margaret, who came from Inishturk, was also the island nurse. She showed me photographs of the island and recommended that I visit if I won the fellowship.

Soon after I went to see the dean of the faculty to ask for a recommendation for the Watson and was shocked to discover that he was Irish. Francis Oakley was in his forties then: a distinguished History of Ideas professor, prematurely white-haired, blue-eyed and cheerful, with a ready smile on his open face. In class he spoke in paragraphs, chapters even, that were as clear as mountain streams and just as effortless. He was President of Williams College from the mid-1980s to the mid-1990s.

It was his English accent that fooled me. Frank, a graduate of Oxford and Yale, was born in Liverpool of Irish parents. His father, Joseph Oakley, came from Athlone. His mother, Siobhán

Curran, was from the tiny village of Ballycasey, near Headford, County Galway, close to Lough Corrib. 'I was surrounded at school by genuine Liverpool Irish, descendants of immigrants who moved there after the Famine,' he said. 'In contrast to their American opposite numbers, they didn't view themselves as Irish, but English – despite their names.' His parents did not regard themselves as immigrants, and always intended to return to Ireland when circumstances improved. 'During the war years,' he said, 'having been brought up to say I was Irish and proud of it, I got into many a fight with schoolmates who viewed the Irish as supporting the Nazis by refuelling German submarines. That, ironically, despite the fact that I was one of the few kids at the school with an English name.'

Frank and Giff recommended me for one of the fellowships. A Williams faculty committee met to nominate four students to compete in the national pool, and I got one of the nominations. Now two hundred undergraduates from fifty colleges all over the United States would compete for seventy fellowships. Faculty support intensified and the pressure mounted. My professor for Modern Jewish Thought, Barbara Nadel, offered to edit my proposal, then grilled me in a mock interview.

Tom MacIntyre's semester at Williams was ending. As he was leaving, he instructed: 'Ring me if you get it. Write to me if you don't.' He gave me a forwarding phone number.

When the Watson cheque for eight thousand dollars arrived in the post some months later, one of the first things I did was to phone MacIntyre. Then I bought a trunk, a portable typewriter, a tweed jacket and a camera, and I enrolled in the 1978 Yeats International Summer School in Sligo. I was the first to arrive at the school and I found myself outside the gates chatting to its affable director, Kevin B. Nowlan. Pat Langan of *The Irish Times* took our photograph, telling me that I reminded him of one of the Kennedys. The photograph appeared in the newspaper the next day. 'I see it didn't take you long to get into *The Irish Times*,' Tom said on the phone from Cavan. It was a happy landing in Ireland.

Alhough I had got off to a good start, the Ireland I came to in 1978 was a country of chronic industrial unrest: there were postal disputes, disruptions of electricity supplies and bus stoppages. I was in sympathy with the strikers; refusing to cross a picket line was in my genes. Adapt to survive, I told myself. I bought a bicycle. I gave my post to anyone heading for America or the North. During the electricity workers' dispute I read Patrick Kavanagh's *The Green Fool* and Brian Moore's *The Lonely Passion of Judith Hearne* by flashlight in my miserable bedsit in Belgrave Square, Monkstown. I wrapped a blanket around my shoulders as the electric heat and lights went out. I endured.

In my more extroverted moments I audited lectures in the Master's programme in Anglo-Irish literature at University College Dublin. I was called 'an occasional student', a phrase I enjoyed. I remember the quiet intensity of Seamus Deane, the geniality and flamboyance of Gus Martin and the decency of Roger McHugh, who was nearing retirement. In the winter of 1978–9 I worked as an intern for the deputy leader of the Labour Party, Michael O'Leary, writing press releases in his office in the Dáil. An evening newspaper asked him to write about a favourite place in Ireland, and I recall his delight when I, having just hitch-hiked all over the north-west, ghost-wrote a piece for him about Donegal. He was witty, charismatic, gifted, distracted and ahead of his time. I was reminded of his energy and charm when I read in May 2006 that he had died suddenly in France.

When I took buses and trains or hitch-hiked around rural Ireland from time to time, I stayed in B&Bs. An old woman in a B&B in Annagry, County Donegal, who was watching Hawaii Five-O on a small television set in the kitchen, came and sat very close to me and told me that she didn't believe that man had landed on the moon. An old man in a B&B in Clifden, County Galway, patted his bald pate after breakfast and shouted at me: 'Why have ye no husband?'

In the summer of 1978 I hitch-hiked to County Cavan to visit MacIntyre, who was staying in the home of his brother, a priest. He instructed me to bring three loaves of brown bread from Bewley's. 'That's Father Noel's dance hall on the right,' the lorry driver told me as we hurtled along towards the village of Doobally, from the Irish *dubh bealach*, 'black way'. Tom was recovering from surgery to remove an epididymal cyst, which would inspire his short story 'The Hospital Barber'. During my visit I noticed a sign in the window of the priest's house, which said: 'Do not open window. Repaired but damaged.' When I pointed out the sign to Tom, he said, 'I'm going to use that line in a radio piece.' In fact, I heard him mention it on *Sunday Miscellany* soon after.

In the spring of 1979 Tom's experimental play *Doobally/Black Way* opened in a theatre in Paris. He was working with an American dance theatre company called Calck Hook, which took its name from an old Dutch neighbourhood in Manhattan, and he actually took part in the performance. I went to the opening of the show and sent a freelance piece to Fergus Linehan in *The Irish Times*. He ran the article, my first for the newspaper, under the heading 'MacIntyre in Paris'.

Back in Dublin, I sat in Bewley's café on Westmoreland Street and read *The Irish Times*. I thought it was a good-looking paper with a liberal ethos, which used photographs well. It was long on opinion, storytelling, features and analysis, and short on the reporting of fact. Some news stories raised more questions than they answered. The word 'I' appeared too often in copy. The features pages could be provocative and the foreign coverage was excellent. The newspaper looked outward to the rest of the world and its world-view was far-reaching, but a permanent move to Ireland was not on my agenda at that time. I faced a more immediate challenge: I had been accepted by the Graduate School of Journalism at Columbia University and was heading to New York. I would remain in Manhattan for the next seven years.

5

CHICKEN NOODLE NEWS

'Good morning, Shirley,' Claus von Bülow said.

'Good morning,' I replied.

My name wasn't Shirley but that didn't matter. It was just another day in Providence, Rhode Island, outside the courtroom where von Bülow was being retried for attempting to murder his multi-millionaire wife, Sunny, by injecting her with insulin. That was how Claus greeted me most mornings, if he used my name at all. It was April 1985. He was the defendant in a second trial for attempted murder because his 1982 conviction by a jury in Newport, Rhode Island, had been overturned on appeal. His new trial had been moved to Providence in an attempt to ensure fairness. I was the CNN producer responsible for the live television coverage of his retrial. I was twenty-eight at the time.

In 1980 Ted Turner had established Cable News Network in Atlanta, Georgia, far from the New York headquarters of the three major networks, NBC, CBS and ABC. His idea had been a highly original one: to create a 24-hour news network emphasising live news coverage from around the world. He was going to challenge the big boys and bring important stories to insular Americans who were being spoon-fed domestic news in half-hour broadcasts.

It was a powerful idea. But when I went to work for CNN in 1983 the network was not yet the player it is today. It was only three years old, a bird in the nest, one the established networks derided as 'Chicken Noodle News'. Its New York bureau was located in the World Trade Center in lower Manhattan, in a glassed-in studio on the ground floor which resembled a goldfish bowl. Tourists and people who worked in the trade centre could stand outside in the lobby, look through the floor-to-ceiling windows and watch the presenters at work under the bright lights. The studio looked glamorous during the day, but at night the office was cold and dark and the assignment editors threw telephone books at mice scampering behind the news desk.

Though it was an architectural icon, I found the World Trade Center a windswept and intimidating place in which to work. I took the subway or a taxi down to work from 5 East 51st Street each day, walked through the crowded lobby and was glad to reach the haven of my desk in the studio behind the bank of news writers and producers. One of the few times I wandered around the massive trade tower, I entered a card shop, stopped to look at a birthday card and promptly had my wallet stolen from my open handbag by a pickpocket. I could feel the wallet slipping away and the immediate sense of violation, but when I turned around no one was there.

My first job was as an assignment editor and for that first year I was always in the office, setting up stories, making contacts, interviewing potential subjects and talking with camera crews in the field on walkie-talkies. I said 'Negative' and '10-4' a lot. There was jargon: 'sound-bites', the quotes or bites from the tape; 'B-roll', or background footage; and 'packages', the name for the finished pieces which were fed to headquarters in Atlanta. The chief assignment editor and I seemed to have a phone permanently attached to our ears. Since it was live, 24-hour television, the deadlines were constant and the situation with breaking news and features was ever-changing. The studio was kept cold for the equipment, which seemed to make us edgy. I needed to wear a jumper all the time, even in summer, although outside on the streets of Manhattan you could fry an egg on the sidewalk. Interesting guests passed though the studio all the time. I never knew who I would see when I looked up from the desk: actors, writers plugging books, financial analysts, people momentarily or permanently in the news, sports figures, politicians and ambassadors. Mayor Ed Koch, who asked everyone he met, 'How'm I doin'?', came in to be interviewed; Daniel J. Travanti from *Hill Street Blues* and New York Governor Mario Cuomo were early interviewees. Benjamin Netanyahu, then Israeli ambassador to the United Nations, was a regular guest in studio. He was always camera-ready and he became a familiar face in the New York bureau of CNN.

Timing was everything. During my first year on the job I rang the Sinn Féin office in Belfast to ask whether Gerry Adams would talk about a breaking story from Northern Ireland. He agreed.

'Mr Adams, please hold.'

The anchorwoman was reading her notes. She was about to go on air when suddenly she called to me across the studio.

'Sheila, how do you pronounce the name of his organisation?'

'Shin Fayne.'

'What does it mean?'

'Ourselves alone.'

Moments later she was live on air and coolly talking to Gerry Adams as though she had been studying Irish politics for years.

CNN moved its New York bureau to more spacious offices on Eighth Avenue between West 33rd and 34th Streets, diagonally opposite Madison Square Garden. During this period I was promoted to writer-producer, a job created for me by the managing editor for the north-east bureau, Jerry Schmetterer, former police bureau chief of the *New York Daily News*. Stocky, bearded, funny and intense, usually gripping a news schedule in his hand, he shouted, 'Where's Sheila?' when news broke.

One morning I arrived at work to find Jerry rushing across the newsroom on the twenty-second floor towards the windows facing uptown Manhattan.

'Where's Sheila?' Jerry roared.

'Here,' I said mildly from a nearby desk, sipping tea from a styrofoam cup. He pulled back the curtains and pointed to a skyscraper on fire about twenty blocks away. It was an image of hell: billowing smoke and angry flames devouring several storeys near the top of the building.

'Go there!'

A camera crew and I left the building immediately and drove towards the burning skyscraper. The police wouldn't let us get too close, but we did get footage of the chaos, the people fleeing, the broken glass, the hoses and the smoke. That's the way it was. When a news story broke, get out of the way. I was gone.

In the new job my brief was to act as an off-camera reporter, interviewing people, reporting and sometimes writing the scripts for the stories, getting the essential shots and B-roll with the camera crews, editing the packages and giving the scripts to on-air people who would do the voice-overs. If there was no time, we handed over the material and let others do the editing and writing. Getting the tapes back to the bureau was the key. You were always in either a CNN van or cameraman's car, or a vehicle hired by CNN to transport tapes and staff. Racing around trying to get tapes back to 5 Penn Plaza was a constant in our lives, a feature of the television news world depicted vividly in the movie *Broadcast News*.

There was a lot more scope for feature stories at CNN than there had been at the *Daily News* and I didn't have to cover as much crime. Every day there was something different, and many of the stories we did were pleasant and absorbing. Most days I was out and about on the streets of New York. One day it was a story about a wheelchair-bound Jimmy Cagney being given the key to the city; the next day it was Harry Belafonte singing 'Hands Across America' to thousands of people at a charity event downtown in Battery Park. I was despatched to Carnegie Hall to interview the Labèque sisters from France, who were seated at two Steinway grand pianos on the stage. I was sent with a list of questions to put to Sean MacBride, who was a very old man at the time. He wore a suit and tie, he sat very still and he had a surprisingly strong French accent. I worked on several packages about 'Art at the United Nations' and stood in awe before Picasso's *Guernica* with a camera crew. I spent weeks on a boat in New York harbour with another crew, gathering footage for an upcoming event at the Statue of Liberty. The statue had been closed for two years for badly-needed restoration work and was reopening on 4 July 1986 as part of the centennial celebration of its dedication in 1886. At the time, the Irish Naval Service was looking for a berth close to the statue, and one of its representatives asked me for help with contacts.

'Ireland has a navy?' Jerry Schmetterer asked.

One sunny day in 1985 a group of CNN staffers were standing around the assignment desk, peering into a computer screen, reading a wire story and shaking their heads in disbelief. They turned to me when they saw me coming.

'Look, Sheila,' Jerry called. 'The Irish have rejected divorce.'

I read the wire copy about the referendum: message from the Stone Age.

I became the New York bureau's unofficial Ireland correspondent. Around this time Tommy Makem and the Clancy Brothers were preparing for their twenty-fifth anniversary reunion concert at Lincoln Center. The camera crew and I went to Tommy Makem's Pavilion on the east side of Manhattan, a beautiful bar lined with framed sketches by Louis le Brocquy, each of which was chained to the white stucco wall. It was startling to see the le Brocquy sketches in an Irish pub, no matter how elegant the east side address. It seemed as if they should have been in a museum of modern art or a private home.

'Ní Shúilleabháin,' Makem said, as he stood beside me, taking my measure. I nodded and told him I had lived in Ireland for a year. He was grave and unusually articulate. I liked his deep voice, his pain and his humour, and his capacity to stand his ground. Makem and Liam Clancy sat for the interview, during which Tommy Makem did most of the talking. He spoke at length about the group's early years when they were collecting folk songs, going to the Lion's Head and dispelling the 'pigs in the kitchen' stereotype of the Irish which prevailed at the time in America. Then he and the Clancys performed 'Brennan on the Moor' and 'Will You Go, Lassie, Go', wearing their trademark Aran sweaters, even though it was a warm summer day and hot under the lights the crew had set up in the pub. The camera rolled. The music was rousing. Their energy, their use of language and their no-holds-barred rendition of Irish songs appealed to Jerry when he looked at the footage back in the studio. CNN let me do the voice-over for the package – the only one I ever voiced with my Boston brogue – and they ran it many, many times in the next 24-hour news cycle. After listening to the tape, someone in Atlanta headquarters asked if I was from Ireland.

'You didn't ask them how much money they made,' Jerry said. He seemed wounded.

'I don't think they know themselves,' I replied.

Waiting is one of the downsides of reporting, whether it's for newspapers, a wire service, radio or television: waiting for press conferences to begin, waiting for statements to be released, waiting for verdicts, waiting for Godot. This was particularly true of the court cases.

When Ariel Sharon sued *Time* magazine for libel, his $50 million suit against what was an almost sacrosanct American institution fascinated the world media. Sharon said that a paragraph published in *Time* falsely suggested that he had encouraged the massacres of hundreds of Palestinians by Christian Phalangist militiamen in the Sabra and Shatila refugee camps in West Beirut in September 1982. At the time, the region was controlled by the Israeli army. Sharon was Israeli Defence

Minister, the man in charge of Israel's invasion and occupation of Lebanon. In 1983 the Israeli Kahan Commission found Sharon indirectly responsible for the slaughter and recommended that he be dismissed from his post. Sharon resigned, but remained in the cabinet without a portfolio.

Sharon called *Time* magazine's 1983 assertion that he encouraged the massacres 'a blood libel' against the Jewish people, and the man known as 'the bulldozer' decided to take on the US media giant in Manhattan Federal District Court.

My role in the coverage was to let the assignment desk know what the six-member jury had decided and keep a phone line open from the federal court building in lower Manhattan to the New York bureau so that CNN could be first on air with the verdict. We waited and waited, and waited and waited, and finally we received word that the jury was coming back. I kept a payphone line open. The jury decided that the information in *Time* was defamatory and false but that the magazine had not published it with reckless disregard for its truth or falsity. Sharon was not successful in proving that he had been libelled but he claimed a moral victory. The decision was unpalatable to both sides. I relayed the verdict to the New York bureau and handed the phone to an on-air correspondent. CNN immediately broadcast the breaking news.

Daily News courtroom artist Joseph Papin had been sitting quietly in court all week, waiting with the rest of us. I don't remember talking to him, but my earnestness and my monopoly of one of the payphones had caught his attention and his satirist's eye. After the verdict was announced and the news conferences ended, he walked over to me and handed me a drawing, an exquisite courtroom sketch done on a large piece of cardboard. Joe must have been working on it while he was waiting for the jury to return; obviously it had taken him a lot of time. It was a caricature of me from the back, standing high up on a bench in a tweed suit and knee-high boots, leaning forward over a crowd of seventeen reporters to catch the words of a smiling Ariel Sharon. A couple of little birds are flitting around me. It exactly caught the flavour and intensity of my days at CNN.

'Climbing after the News' at Trial of Time vs Sharon
Federal Court Manhattan Jan 24, 1985
Shortly before the final verdict we see Sheila standing head and shoulders above all the rest (as usual) in being first for the facts!! Congratulations! Sheila.
Woe to any artwork left lying in the way.
Joe Papin

I remembered Joe Papin's cartoon fifteen years later, in September 2000. While working on the *Irish Times* foreign desk, I monitored wire service reports about the intention of Sharon, then Israel's opposition leader, to visit the Al-Aqsa mosque compound on Temple Mount in Jerusalem. As the days passed and opposition to Sharon's impending visit grew, I read our correspondent's copy and agency stories with increasing dread. Sharon insisted on making the visit and the second Palestinian *intifada*, or uprising, began.

The von Bülow retrial in the spring of 1985 would prove to be the biggest challenge I had at CNN. It was one of the first US media circuses, only the second trial in American history to be televised live, gavel-to-gavel, and this time I had a major job to do as producer of CNN's live coverage. The case inspired a movie, *Reversal of Fortune*, starring Jeremy Irons as Claus von Bülow and Glenn Close as the doomed Sunny. It was based on the book by Alan Dershowitz, the lawyer who masterminded the overturning of von Bülow's conviction on appeal.

Producing the trial coverage meant staying for three months in the Biltmore Hotel in Providence and commuting to New York from Rhode Island at the weekend. CNN would fly us back and forth. I had a corner suite in the stately old hotel, and I was there for so long that I rearranged the furniture in the suite. We worked on that trial coverage morning, noon and night, and when I went back to the hotel it was to order shrimp cocktails from room service, fill out expense forms and get some sleep. It was good to be in Providence, an old city by American standards, which was in some respects a smaller version of Boston, slowly undergoing a process of urban renewal. It was spring and the balmy weather and the bright evenings in the city reminded me of my childhood in Chelsea, but there wasn't time to stop and smell the roses. I spent most of my waking hours between the courtroom and a satellite truck parked outside the courthouse from which we would feed the tape and do live shots.

The CNN correspondent assigned to cover the trial was Charles Feldman, a Brooklyn-born television reporter with a resonant voice, a refined on-air presence and an attachment to Manhattan so strong that he had a particular distaste for leaving it. The camera 'man' and the sound 'man' were young women, a novel state of affairs even in those pioneering days. They were cheerful and able, but the camera woman was so short that she had to stand on a stepladder to get shots of von Bülow, who was over six feet tall. She and her partner lugged the camera, the heavy tripod, the sound equipment and the stepladder around without complaint.

'Chicken Noodle News,' the burly cameramen from the big networks, wearing jackets and baseball caps with company logos, muttered under their breath.

People were watching us. Four hundred thousand viewers a day were hooked on the von Bülow coverage, and Charles and I were pulling out all the stops to provide coverage that was occupying most of CNN's daytime schedule. The retrial coverage was raising CNN's profile, and the bosses in Atlanta liked what we were doing and gave us airtime and a lot of room in which to manoeuvre.

The prosecutors alleged that Claus had injected his wife with insulin to inherit her money and marry his 'mistress', soap opera actress Alexandra Isles. We wanted to know if Alexandra was going to testify. At one point Ms Isles was believed to be living in Ireland and Charles and I phoned a number in Blackrock, County Dublin, looking for her, but to no avail. The defence team argued that Sunny's own self-destructive behaviour, her drinking and alleged drug use, had resulted in her coma.

Lesson number one: the prosecutors may have been trying to prove what really happened to Mrs von Bülow, who was lying in Columbia Presbyterian Hospital in an irreversible coma, but the defence team's goal was to establish reasonable doubt and win the case.

Charles Feldman spoke beautifully on air, explaining medical testimony in layman's terms each weekday for eleven weeks; it was a performance I could only watch in awe. There was complicated evidence about insulin and comas but he made it simple. Even when the jury went for its deliberations, we stayed on the air and kept working, with Charles interviewing some of the well-known journalists attending the trial.

The retrial of Claus von Bülow was all we did, all the time. The ever-growing media pack ate together every night and sometimes news broke as a result of those gatherings, at which information was shared. There was curiosity about Claus's constant companion, a Hungarian woman named Andrea Reynolds, who was referred to in the newspapers as 'thrice-married'. 'Check the labels on Andrea's jacket if you can. See if she's wearing Sunny's clothes,' a colleague whispered to me at one of these dinners.

Beside me in the courtroom for much of those eleven weeks was an older man with sad eyes and the most expensive ties I had ever seen. One day in court he spoke to me. 'I hear you went to Williams.'

'Yes.'

'I did too. I knew I liked you.'

I smiled. Writer Dominick Dunne, a former Hollywood producer, was covering the von Bülow retrial for *Vanity Fair* magazine. He was the brother of John Gregory Dunne (1932–2003), who was the author of *True Confessions* and the husband of writer Joan Didion. Born in Hartford, Connecticut, in 1925, Dominick was the son of heart surgeon Dr Richard E. Dunne and Dorothy Burns Dunne. There was an Irish link: his maternal grandfather, Dominick Burns, was born in Roscommon. Dominick graduated from Williams College in 1949 and spent twenty-five years in Hollywood, where, it seemed, he had met and known everybody: he was a close friend of Elizabeth Taylor and he greeted Lauren Bacall as 'Betty'.

He had suffered a great tragedy. In 1982 his 22-year-old daughter Dominique, an actress who appeared in the movie *Poltergeist*, went into a coma after being strangled by her former boyfriend, John Sweeney. She never regained consciousness, was taken off life support and died. When I met Dominick in 1985 he was still wearing that grief. Sweeney, the former boyfriend, had been sentenced to six years for Dominique's death, and the jail term was automatically reduced to three on the day of sentencing. He got out of prison in two-and-a-half years with time served. In 1984 Dominick wrote a piece about his daughter's trial for *Vanity Fair* at the urging of its new editor, Tina Brown. 'Justice: A Father's Account of his Daughter's Killer' began a new stage in his career which, Dominick himself would admit, eventually amounted to an obsession with reporting and writing about rich and famous people who were accused of murder.

No stone was left unturned, no detail deemed insignificant by the media, if it pertained to the main participants in the von Bülow case.

'What do you know about the judge?' Dominick asked me one day. There had been speculation about the woman judge, Corrine Grande, and how she would handle the case.

Dominick and I used to get to court early to get good seats and that morning we were the first to arrive. I told him that the judge had summoned CNN's camera woman to her chambers, and I had been concerned that she was going to exclude our camera for some reason. But no, the judge wanted to know how she was coming across on television. She knew that she was on air a good deal during the live feed. She asked about camera angles and how she looked wearing her eyeglasses. Charles said she even sought advice about make-up.

Dominick was stunned and, as always, he began to take notes on a small pad, which seemed to appear out of nowhere.

'What do *you* know about the judge?' I asked him in turn.

He told me what little he had heard. She apparently still lived at home with her mother and he had seen her father sitting in court, watching the proceedings.

'Is that the man who looks like he's wearing a toupée?' I asked.

'I think so.'

Now I have no idea whether in fact Judge Grande lived with her mother, and for all we knew her father might have had a fine head of his own hair. This was just the idle conversation of the working press on that particular morning in court.

'So,' I said. 'She lives with her mother, and her father wears a rug.'

Dominick roared with laughter as we stood outside the courtroom. His laugh came from somewhere deep. His shoulders shook, and when his laughter began to subside, it started up again. He wrote down the line in his notebook. In later years he went on to write many novels, including *The Two Mrs Grenvilles*, *An Inconvenient Woman* and *People Like Us*, all of which were made into mini-series for television. In 1993 his novel *A Season in Purgatory* was published and made into a mini-series. In the novel I came upon a scene in which two men were talking:

> 'Have you been able to get any information on the judge?' asked Jerry.
>
> 'She lives with her mother, and her father wears a rug,' said Eddie Bargetta.

I phoned Dominick.

'It is my *hommage* to you,' he said.

The retrial ended in Claus's acquittal and most of the national press corps prepared to go home, exhausted. The long weeks of work and pressure had taken their toll on our energy. After the verdict Charles went to the hospital in Providence complaining of shortness of breath. When I took a taxi to go and check on him, I felt as if I should be admitted also.

CNN management sent us thank-you letters and gave us both a week off with pay. The following year a CNN executive in Atlanta was awarded a National Headliner Award for consistently outstanding TV news reporting by a network: among the stories cited was the von Bülow retrial coverage, during which, the citation said, 'CNN continued its commitment to provide the public with a unique opportunity to witness first-hand the judicial system at work.' A photocopy of a letter about the awards dinner, which was attended by an executive from the New York bureau, was left on my desk in Manhattan while I was out on assignment.

Dominick Dunne continues to write for *Vanity Fair* magazine.

Sunny von Bülow is still in a coma. She has been moved from Columbia Presbyterian Hospital in New York to a private nursing home on the Upper East Side.

The *Daily Telegraph* reported in May 2004 that Claus von Bülow had been appointed contributing editor at the *Catholic Herald* in London after serving for two years as the paper's drama critic.

6

'Walking in Snow'

Marjorie Alma Parker, née Winn, sat in her kitchen in Auckland, New Zealand, and told a local newspaper reporter: 'If I hear that piece of music one more time I think I'm going to go out of my mind.' Marjorie had been trying to write her gardening column while her son Brent played the piano in the next room.

Brent was born in Christchurch, New Zealand, in January 1933. He began to study piano at the age of nine and displayed a remarkable ability at the keyboard. At fifteen, while he was a student at Christchurch Boys' High, he was offered a year's free tuition in London by a visiting examiner. Marjorie's brother, Reg Winn, offered to take him to England, but his teacher, Ernest Empson, went to Brent's house and told Marjorie, 'The Royal Academy of Music churns out two hundred mediocre students each year.' So Brent didn't go to London.

Marjorie and her husband, Selwyn Parker, an insurance salesman, moved their family of four children to Auckland, on the North Island, when Brent was eighteen. He toured the north of New Zealand with violinist Sam Artis from the London Symphony Orchestra and soprano Honor McKellar. In 1952 he took the performers' diploma exam, the LRSM (Licentiate of the Royal Schools of Music, London). The day after the exam he played Beethoven's second piano concerto in B flat major with the Auckland Radio Orchestra in a competition in which he came second. He was practising up to eleven hours a day at the time.

Brent studied harmony with Georg Tintner, the great Bruckner conductor, who was born in Vienna in 1917. Tintner, who was Jewish, escaped the Nazis in 1938 and settled in New Zealand for a time. Brent said Georg Tintner 'was a type of musician beyond my experience. When conducting he could sing horn parts when players went astray. He could name notes accurately, unseen and bashed out by myself on a keyboard.' Tintner once told a reviewer:

> The worse our age becomes, the more we need music that consoles: music that is full of repose, and is restful in itself. There is space for Bruckner and for Mahler, but for the opposite reasons. Mahler was the prophet of angst and horror, whereas Bruckner transcends this condition.

Long hours practising the piano began to cause Brent muscular problems. Around this time, in the early 1950s, he discovered a teacher, Frank Cooper, who knew about these conditions, and Brent studied the release of involuntary tensions with him for about two years. Frank's exercises helped Brent to achieve muscular relaxation; this process, in turn, improved the tone he produced at the piano. Brent describes Frank Cooper as 'a philosopher-composer and a teacher of piano technique who could play any instrument except the harp, and whose practical application was unique and still is'. As a composer of operas, Frank was interested in going abroad in search of opera houses in Europe. In the summer of 1956 Frank decided to leave New Zealand, and Brent, aged twenty-three, went with him.

Frank, Brent and two other pianists named Randy and Bruno boarded the Orient Line's *Otranto*, bound for France via the Suez Canal. The trip took nearly five weeks. The ship called into Sydney, Adelaide, Melbourne, Freemantle and Perth, Colombo in Ceylon (now Sri Lanka), Aden, Port Said and Naples. The musicians disembarked in Marseilles. 'All piano lessons ceased due to no piano being available, and most eating stopped due to no money being available,' Brent recalls.

Brent contracted tuberculosis and spent six months in hospital in London, where he was visited by a representative of the New Zealand embassy and was cared for by an Irish nurse, Cecilia Power, who told him about an opera house in Cork. Once Brent had recovered sufficiently, the group of pianists headed for Ireland.

Frank may have been an expert in releasing involuntary tension, but he had not done his homework on the political situation in Ireland. When the Kiwis arrived, they didn't even know that the Border existed. They arrived in a poor country, priest-ridden and damp. 'The conditions for becoming a concert pianist didn't improve,' Brent said.

'What is there in this country for this young man?' Gay Byrne wondered aloud on the *Late Late Show* when Brent played for him in the mid-1960s.

The musicians left Cork and landed in Bray, County Wicklow. Eventually Brent married and had children, and the group of pianists dispersed. Frank Cooper died and was buried in Brighton, England; the others returned to New Zealand.

Ireland remained priest-ridden, poor and damp, but Brent had a young, growing family to support. For three years in the 1960s he drove a bus for CIÉ. His milk bill was almost as much as his weekly wages. During his lunch break in the bus depot in Donnybrook he looked up at a patch of blue in the grey Dublin sky and he raged. At home at night he began to write music, using a drawing-board made from a piece of timber. With a pencil and a pile of blank paper, he wrote a piano concerto inspired by the Hungarian Uprising of 1956, which had occurred in the year he left New Zealand. Hardship in Ireland had turned him into a composer.

The 1970s were better for him. He got work as a part-time

teacher at the College of Music, which was then in Chatham Row. He played his *Piano Concerto No 1 in G major* with the RTÉ Symphony Orchestra, in a performance conducted by Proinsias Ó Duinn, in a recorded rehearsal in the St Francis Xavier Hall. There was no National Concert Hall in Dublin at the time.

He wrote a second piano concerto, which he performed with the RTÉ Symphony Orchestra and which was conducted by Colman Pearse. That work was broadcast on RTÉ. Pianist Ethna Tinney played his *French Variations* in the Hugh Lane Gallery, Dublin. He worked with John Barry on the film *The Lion in Winter*, which was being shot in County Wicklow, rehearsing Katharine Hepburn as a singer. Classical guitarist John Feeley commissioned him to write guitar concertos, which he and Brent played many times. By this stage, performances of Brent's music had been heard in Ireland, America, France and Greece.

He was hired as a full-time teacher in the College of Music, which is now known as the Dublin Institute of Technology Conservatory of Music and Drama. He remained there for almost twenty years.

'Mr Parker?'

I opened the door of the music room in the college on Adelaide Road, Dublin, and found a 59-year-old man with two pianos, standing in the sunlight with his hands in his pockets, relaxed and composed. He was over six feet tall, with grey hair turning white. His expression was genial and his blue-eyed gaze was alert. The two pianos – a Petrof upright and a Steinway baby grand – almost filled the room. A piece of music hung on the wall over the baby grand.

'What's that?' I asked. I took a closer look: 'The Monks of Glendalough', one of his own compositions. Written by hand, it was adorned with the history of musical notation. It was an art object, like an illuminated manuscript, as well as a piece of music.

'I'll play it for you.' He sat down at the Steinway.

The music sounded like a prayer.

'How do you feel about Chopin?' I had asked when Brent rang a few weeks earlier to schedule my first lesson.

'Chopin is the reason I became a musician.'

It was September 1992. I had bought a piano and auditioned to become a mature student in the DIT College of Music.

'You did a lot of work as a child, didn't you,' the nun who examined me said quietly. Instantly I was back with Sister Olivia in the light-filled auditorium in Boston, a little girl in a yellow dress playing *Fantasie Impromptu*, with people clapping and clapping and the saintly, elderly nun backstage telling me she loved me. I was accepted as a mature piano student and assigned to Brent.

'Oh, everybody wants him,' a colleague told me.

'He's a good composer and a good teacher,' a neighbour said.

When I arrived for my second lesson I heard an oboe playing a long, soulful note. 'What's that?'

'My first piano concerto.'

Your first piano concerto – were there more? I wondered. I tried to remember the definition of a concerto but I had been away from music studies for a long time.

Brent said he had played the concerto himself in a recorded rehearsal with the RTÉ Symphony Orchestra. It told the story of a young pianist on the eve of the 1956 Hungarian Uprising in Budapest. He offered to make a copy for me if I brought a blank cassette tape to my next lesson.

At home after my second lesson, I looked up the word concerto in my 1978 *American Heritage Dictionary*: 'a composition for an orchestra and one or more solo instruments, typically in three movements'. Then I looked up New Zealand: 'An independent member of the Commonwealth of Nations, 103,416 square miles in area, in the Pacific Ocean about 1,200 miles south-east of Australia. It comprises North Island, South Island, and several smaller adjacent islands. Population: 2,815,000. Capital: Wellington.'

I brought in a blank cassette tape for my third lesson. At my fourth lesson, Brent gave me a copy of his piano concerto and I took it home. While fifteen-month-old Conor slept upstairs, I sat in my living room and listened to the work, and was surprised to find myself moved. I had been away from the company of other pianists for more than fifteen years; memories stirred. The recording of the concerto was a little scratchy but the music was well crafted and descriptive, romantic and emotional. The melodies were lyrical. It was unapologetically music for middlebrows. Brent's playing was that of a virtuoso, all flying fingers, crashing chords and tidal hands. In the first movement I could hear the tanks, the second movement inspired reverie and the third restored normality. The pianist was the hero soloist pitted against the authoritarian force of the orchestra.

My favourite moment was the first note of the piano in the middle movement, a note of nostalgia. I felt that the work was about the love of one's own land, whether that land was Hungary or New Zealand or America. After so many years in the breaking news business, this was a more emotional experience than I had anticipated. 'I think it should be performed live,' I announced when I arrived for my fifth lesson. 'It's crazy to leave a piece like that in a drawer.'

Brent looked at me. 'Have you practised your scales?' he asked.

'No.'

He looked down.

'If you could choose, who would you like to conduct your concerto?' I asked.

'Robert Houlihan.' Brent was referring to a regular guest conductor of the National Symphony Orchestra in Dublin who had conducted for the GPA Piano Competition. 'One of my students knows him. I think he lives in France.'

'Get me his address if you can, please.' And then I sat down at the Petrof to play a piece of Schubert.

'You're hitting the wrong note there and it's driving me crazy,'

Brent cried, pointing to the music.

Over the Christmas break Brent went home and resurrected his concerto. He copied it out by hand, a process which took an entire month.

I wrote a letter to Robert Houlihan in Metz, France. It turned out that the Kerry-born maestro was the principal conductor and artistic director of the Savaria Symphony Orchestra from Szombathely, in north-west Hungary, which happens to be the birthplace of Leopold Bloom's father in *Ulysses*.

To my astonishment, Robert Houlihan, known as Bobby to his friends, phoned me at home a short time after receiving my letter to say that he and his orchestra 'would be delighted' to perform a concerto based on the Hungarian Uprising of 1956.

At my next lesson I told Brent about the call from Bobby.

'You are a ray of light.'

'You are a lucky man to be so talented.'

He looked pained. Being a composer had not been easy. It emerged that there had been one previous attempt, by Brent's mother, to have his first piano concerto performed in New Zealand by a conductor called Juan Matteucci. In a letter to Brent from Auckland, posted 24 July 1977, Marjorie Parker wrote:

> You will recently have received that huge epistle from me. I posted it on the way to the Symphonia where, after a wait, I intercepted Juan Matteucci as he came in. I'll spare you the finer details but will tell you that they were amusing when I thought back on them.
>
> He speaks quite broken English and talks with his hands as well. I didn't realise it at the time but – I 'do same'. Here we were like two Latins rehearsing a love scene. Well, Brent, I was absolutely overcome as this had never entered my head for a moment. At first I did not quite take it in and then the penny

dropped – he wants you to come to New Zealand next year to play your own concerto. Expenses paid. He say again, 'Vunderful vunderful music and only Brent can play it from zee 'art.' Expressing meanwhile with two hands pressed to 'zee 'art.'

As a music student Brent saw Matteucci guest-conduct the New Zealand Symphony Orchestra in Auckland sometime between 1951 and 1956. Matteucci was awe-inspiring.

'He was very big on the stage and had immense style in dress and movement. He had a very thin waist and wore a tailored black suit.

'He looked like a large black beetle from behind, with long, expressive arms, and was in total command,' Brent said. 'At that time I had no notion of ever writing any music whatsoever.'

Juan Matteucci died before arrangements could be made to fly Brent to New Zealand to play his concerto with the Auckland Symphonia, and the piano concerto went back in the drawer.

My piano lessons continued through the grey Dublin winter.

One day in March 1993, when I didn't have my car, Brent offered to give me a lift home after my lesson. We walked out through the back of the College of Music, went around past the traditional music pub, An Béal Bocht, and headed towards the Charlemont bridge over the canal. It began to snow, and I looked up. It was a rare flurry in Dublin and large white flakes were sticking to the ground.

'It reminds me of Boston,' I said.

Brent smiled.

The snow was coming faster now. I picked up the pace, striding happily now, heading for the bridge, and Brent kept in time with me. I looked around us. The Barge pub was on our right. The Ranelagh road was ahead of us. The snow had transformed the dreary city into a luminous white film set.

'It looks like a movie,' I said.

Sheila's father, Frederick Sullivan, reading the *Chelsea Record* at home in Chelsea, Massachusetts, in the 1970s.

Sheila with her mother and sister Kathleen in her aunt's house in Braintree, Massachusetts, before her wedding in 1983.

Jimmy Breslin at his home in Forest Hills, Queens, New York, in the early 1980s.

Bob Lane interviewing New York Congresswoman Bella Abzug
for the *Daily News* in the 1970s.

Sheila with Claus von Bülow outside the courthouse in Providence, Rhode Island, in 1985.

Sheila's New York press pass
when she worked for the *Daily News*.

Tom MacIntyre performing with American
dance theatre company Calck Hook in a Paris
production of his play *Doobally/Black Way* in 1979.

Sheila and her sister Kathleen with Massachusetts Governor Michael Dukakis, Democratic presidential candidate in 1988, at Kathleen's wedding in Boston in 1989.

Sheila with a CNN camera crew on assignment in the mid-1980s.

Sketch of Sheila by John Behan, drawn on Inishbofin, County Galway,
after the death of her father in 1981.

Brent Parker at the piano
Top: Linenhall, Castlebar, County Mayo (2004)
Bottom: St Thomas's Church, Dugort, Achill (2003). (Photo: Ken Wright)

Conor at a John Behan exhibition in Dublin in 1995.

Sheila's house in Dookinella, Achill. (Photo: Emmanuel Prolat)

Mrs Violet McDowell, of Gray's Guest House, Dugort, Achill.

We crossed the bridge and headed towards his car, which was parked by the canal. I was captivated by the falling snow, with Brent in step beside me. He was looking at me, thinking. In my mind I was back in Chelsea, walking over Powder Horn Hill. The land on the hill, said to have been traded by Native Americans to early settlers for a powder horn, was covered in snow. I used to walk over that hill on my way home from school. My father had expressed mild concern about my long-legged stride, which was quite similar to his own, and he had tried a few times in vain to get me to take smaller steps, to make my walk more 'ladylike'. 'I don't want you to look like a longshoreman,' he used to say, an expression inspired by the nearby Boston Navy Yard in Charlestown, which my parents pronounced in the Irish way, with three syllables: Char-les-town. 'Shape up or ship out' was another expression from the navy yard, but more often I heard, 'I don't want you to walk like a longshoreman.'

Too late now, Daddy: I was loping across Charlemont bridge with Brent. The windscreen of his car was covered in snow. He cleared it and he drove me home.

After my lesson the following week Brent said, 'I've written a piece of music.'

I was puzzled. I thought he was going to tell me again that my tone on the Schubert was terrible.

'It's called "Walking in Snow".'

He showed me the piano score: the notes were drawn by hand in the same beautiful way as they had been for 'The Monks of Glendalough', which hung on the wall over the piano in his music room at the college. I studied the music. The composer's instruction was *Andantino* – in a moderately slow tempo.

'It's the rhythm of your walk.'

How about that, Daddy? My longshoreman's walk had inspired a song.

In a composer's note about the piece, Brent wrote:

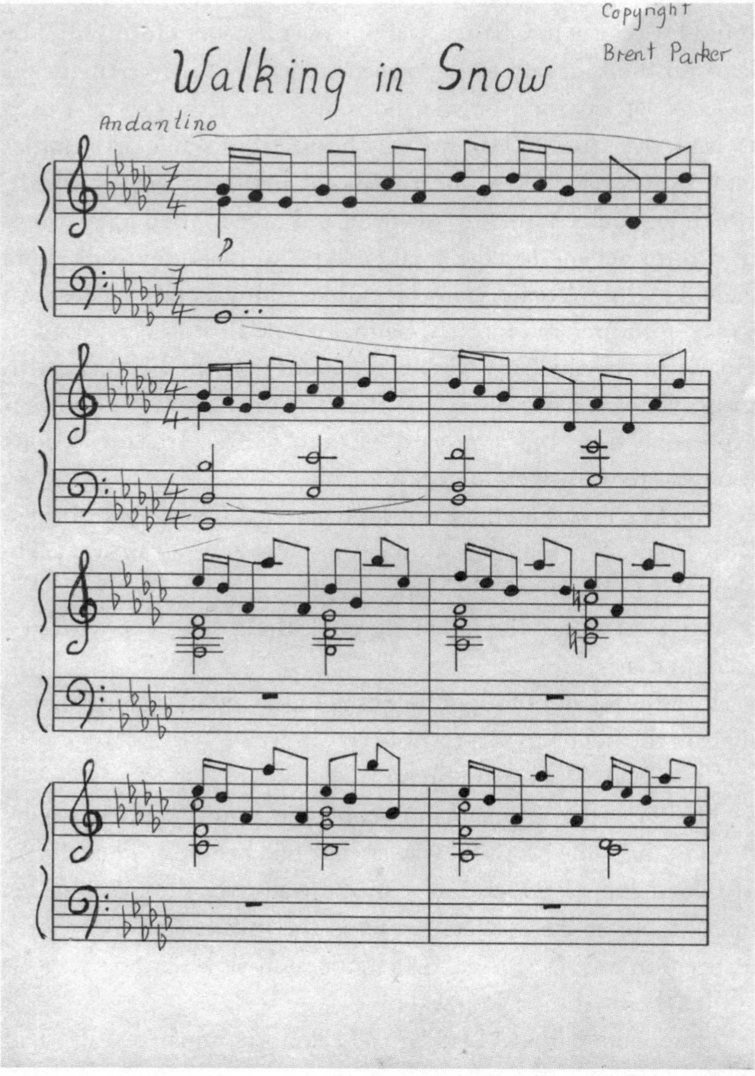
Walking in Snow
Copyright
Brent Parker
Andantino
p

This is about a fine step tiptoeing through the snow being watched and accompanied by the composer. The delicate demeanour of the owner of the fine step entranced and bewildered the observer. Some way through he moves to the other side of the fine step to make sure it was true. It was true and the composer created 'Walking in Snow' the next day and, in doing so, discovered himself to anyone listening. It starts with the fine step; continues with the appreciation of the fine step; and melts with love. The original is for piano and is in G flat major, a key of much romance.

He played the piece for me, and as he did, I felt the joy of crossing the bridge in Ranelagh with the snow on my face. Walking in snow. Falling in love? Same number of syllables.

Brent played a cassette tape of 'Walking in Snow' for Bach scholar Dr Joseph Groocock in his car one Thursday night when he gave him a lift home from the College of Music in Chatham Row.

'You may have a winner there,' Dr Groocock said.

The following year, in August 1994, my mother died of breast cancer. I was thirty-eight. She had been diagnosed seven years earlier after the discovery of a lump under her arm. Her cancer had not been detected early and had spread to her lymph system, but her team at Massachusetts General Hospital managed the case well and gave her more time. After a mastectomy and treatment, she enjoyed several good years in retirement, spending her summers on Cape Cod with my brother John and her winters looking after Kathy's twin boys, Matthew and Patrick, and daughter Megan. In the end the doctors could only do what they could do.

A young and inexperienced mother at twenty-one, she had weighed her first-born on the scales, crying if the baby lost an ounce or two, although the doctor tried to reassure her that those fluctuations were perfectly normal. Now she herself was so thin: eight stone three and slender as a girl at the age of sixty-eight. She was fading away.

When we were children and it snowed heavily, she was the one who phoned the local radio stations to call off school. The superintendent, Mr Herlihy, would phone her with his decision and she would notify the stations. 'Twenty-two. No school,' she'd say, giving the code so they would know it was not a hoax. It snowed so much in Boston that sometimes there would be no school for a week and our lives were transformed: the old grey city would disappear under a beautiful white blanket. When we woke up after a major storm, we listened outside my mother's bedroom door for the magic words: 'Twenty-two. No school.' After shovelling out the cars and clearing the sidewalks we'd use our sleds and toboggans, throw snowballs or build snowmen in the backyard. We'd come home, frozen but exhilarated, take off our boots in the back hall and go down to the basement to remove our coats, scarves, hats, mittens and wet trousers.

On the day before my mother died I flew from Dublin to Boston with Conor, who was three. We sat on the ground at Dublin Airport for several hours, caught in an Aer Lingus dispute, with Conor squirming and crawling up my face. When I arrived at my sister's house in Brookline, Massachusetts, my mother was dying on a white bed covered in a soft white duvet and pillows, with a dark-haired hospice nurse from Roscommon by her side. She died overnight, in the early hours. Twenty-two. No school.

Three months later, on 19 November 1994, my estranged husband Bob asked if he could have a word with me at the paper. We had separated and sold our house in May 1994, but we both still worked in the newsroom of *The Irish Times*. It was a strain. He told me he was leaving for America the next day for one month. His mind appeared to be made up, his leave was arranged, and while several colleagues were aware of his plans, I hadn't known.

Bob remained in America for eighteen months and during that time I had no idea if he was ever coming back.

'My wedding dress is in a dry-cleaner's in Dublin,' I said. I lay in the brass bed I had shipped in a container from New York to Cork nine years before, along with my oil painting of Sean O'Casey, my Villeroy and Boch porcelain dinner plates with floral pattern, my rocking chair with Williams College insignia, my extra-large American ironing board, my tape cassette of *Appalachian Spring* by Aaron Copland, my term paper on *Moby-Dick* entitled 'The Whiteness of the Whale', and forty boxes of other worldly goods and chattels, bound tightly in bubble-packing.

'It was a nice dress,' I said, looking out the bedroom window. It was late November 1995 in Ireland, and the afternoon was dark and dank. It felt as though someone had put a lid over the country to keep in the rain and the damp and the wind. The glands at the back of my neck were swollen and stiff, my nightgown was soaked with sweat and my sheets were damp from night fever. My forehead hurt and I had a tight feeling in my chest. When the phone rang, it was as if a fire alarm had gone off in the silence of my long illness. I didn't have the strength to get out of bed to answer it, so I slowly reached over and placed the receiver on my pillow and moved my head to reach the mouthpiece.

'I bought it at Henri Bendel in New York,' I told Pat Harris. 'It had a long satin train, a high neck and dozens of tiny buttons up the back.'

'It must have been stunning,' Pat said, in a slightly Anglicised Irish accent. 'I wish I could have seen it.' Her doorbell rang, and she said 'Sorry' a bit irritably and went to answer it. I leaned back on the firm, king-size mattress and waited, looking longingly at a clean, dry, white cotton nightgown lying folded on a wicker chair at the bottom of my bed. The nightgown, a souvenir from Paradise Island, had 'It's Better in the Bahamas' in aquamarine letters across the front. I could not disagree. I wondered whether

I had the energy to change into it, and decided I did not. Pat said sharply, 'What do you want?' to someone at her front door, but I couldn't hear the mumbled male reply.

I sank back on my pillow and recalled the white lace and little pearls, the shock and magic of my wedding-dress, and the peace and sun-lit splendour of Henri Bendel's dressing room on Fifth Avenue. After buying the dress I had walked a couple of blocks to Bergdorf Goodman for the shoes, white cloth with a medium heel.

My wedding day in Boston – 9 April 1983 – had been preceded by an ungodly downpour. On the eve of the wedding the rain was torrential and road conditions were treacherous for the arriving guests. In an uncharacteristic gesture, I placed rosary beads on my windowsill as a last-ditch appeal to the divine for an end to the rain.

On the morning of my wedding I rose at five to iron a pile of clothes I didn't need. By six the sun was shining – brilliantly. At eight the groom phoned and sang 'Oh, what a beautiful mornin'…' in his baritone voice. At nine I dressed and the florist arrived with a garland for my hair. At ten I was driven by limousine to Our Lady of Grace, the large granite church in Chelsea, Massachusetts, on the Everett border, where I had been baptised. Three ushers, all Vietnam veterans, waited on the steps, dressed in grey morning suits, smiling and chatting to my great-aunt Louise Carney, who was resplendent in a coral-blue dress, mink stole and sensible shoes.

I walked towards the altar on the arms of both brothers – John, bearded and blue-eyed, and Freddie, tall and brown-eyed like my father. As we moved towards the altar, smiling at the ninety-six guests on both sides of the aisle who were leaning towards us and smiling back, my heart pounded and my eyes watered at the music. In the organ loft, my friend Brian McConville from Dorchester, then a conducting student at Yale, was playing one of his own compositions.

Father Broderick, who had celebrated Mass at my First Communion, emerged on the altar wearing large, rectangular, tinted eyeglasses. He said, 'You look lovely, my dear,' which I had found odd. I remembered the way the same priest had banged open the wooden partition in the confessional following my First Confession nearly twenty years before, turned his head ninety degrees, and looked straight into my startled little face. He hadn't been supposed to do that either. He was full of surprises, I thought, as the groom nudged the gold wedding ring over my knuckle.

The limousine took us over the Mystic River Bridge into downtown Boston, to the Ritz Carlton Hotel in Copley Square. A maître-d' greeted us at the door. 'Mrs Lane,' he said in an Irish accent, nodding slightly. Charmed that he was the first person to use my married name, I asked him where he was from. 'Galway,' he replied, smiling, with another nod.

I stood by myself in the Ritz ballroom, looking out the tall windows at the April sun on the trees in Boston Public Garden, my back turned to the guests, a loner bride of twenty-six thinking with the back of my head. Kathy, auburn-haired and smiling, in a long yellow dress with yellow and bluish-purple flowers in her hair, helped me with my train. The wedding photographer tugged my arm a little too hard and Freddie whispered in my ear, 'Just think of yourself as a bolt of cloth.' As we posed for photographs in the magnificent ballroom, another guest strode up to where the wedding party was standing and said she had locked her American Express card inside her suitcase. I felt a slight rush of adrenalin. 'Don't worry about it,' Kathy said to me in a low voice.

My mother, fine-featured and slender at fifty-six, wore a knee-length mauve dress with a matching flower in her hair. My father had died two years earlier. This was her first major occasion since his funeral and she had organised the wedding with energy and precision. There were logistical challenges: I lived in New York and she lived in Chelsea. There were so many details, so little time.

I was asked to make decisions on matters about which I had no opinion: china or porcelain, steak or fish, chowder or vichyssoise, long tablecloths or short? 'Would you like the harp?' the Ritz wedding planner had asked. I remained silent. My mother paused. 'I like the harp,' she said.

Now waiters were pouring champagne into blue glasses on white linen tablecloths that reached to the floor. The orchestra played. It was a rare day in Boston, and as Bob and I danced my mother surveyed the scene with satisfaction.

'Here I am,' Pat Harris said, returning to the phone, rasping slightly. She was a chain-smoker who suffered from emphysema. 'That was the Telecom repair man. Sorry. Now, where were we? Where is your wedding-dress, did you say?'

'Craft Cleaners on Upper Baggot Street.' I relaxed a little. Talking to Pat Harris was like stepping into a warm bath. When we met I had been impressed by her elegance and directness of speech. She was an elderly widow with an erect carriage but frail physique, the kind of stalwart older woman with a huge amount of mental energy but not enough accompanying physical strength. Obviously she had been a great beauty. Her age was unfathomable but I guessed she was in her late seventies. Clever, artistic and appropriately vain, her hauteur was tempered by humour. She lived in Northcote Road, Dún Laoghaire, in a two-storey house which she called Ibsen because it reminded her of a doll's house. She had driven an ambulance for the Red Cross in London during the Second World War. She had run her own curtain business on the south side of Dublin. She had been married twice and I found her worldly-wise and exciting, in a Katherine Hepburn, stiff-upper-lip kind of way. It always cheered me when she phoned during my long illness.

'Do you intend to redeem your wedding dress after all this time? Try to salvage it perhaps?'

'No. I intend to try to salvage myself.'

'Have you any news from the doctor?'

'Not lately. Not since he gave me more antibiotics.'

'How many courses of antibiotics have you been on?'

'I've actually lost count. Five, maybe six.'

'Are you still bedridden?'

'Virtually.'

'How long have you been ill now?'

'Sixteen weeks.'

And there had been no improvement really. Overnight my chest had hurt so much, I had been so weak and my temperature had been so high that I had lain absolutely still, looking straight at the wall and listening to myself, as I had seen seriously-ill hospital patients do. I had managed to remove my damp nightgown, which felt as though someone had run it under the tap, and put on a clean, dry nightshirt, which had 'I love New York' in red letters on the front. Eventually I'd fallen back to sleep. When I awoke the next morning, my fever had broken.

'Does your husband know how ill you are?' Pat asked.

'No.'

'Where is he?'

'In New York or New Jersey, I guess.'

'Has he phoned?'

'No.'

'How long has he been away?'

'Eighteen months.'

'Is he coming back?'

'I don't know,' I said testily. I hated the question.

'What do you tell your son?'

'The truth – that I don't know.'

Pat paused. 'And how is your son?'

'The cherub is asleep.'

The truth was that I was concerned about Conor. His father was gone, his grandmother had died and his mother was ill, and he hadn't asked for any of this. He had brought such joy when he was born on 11 June 1991 in Mount Carmel Hospital. It was a warm summer evening and I could see the Dublin mountains from the delivery room. Dr Karl Mullen appeared, wearing a big smile and a pair of yellow boots.

'Why the K in Karl?' I had asked during my first visit to his rooms.

'My father named me for Karl Marx.'

Minutes after Karl appeared, Conor arrived too, as surely and steadily as a wave of the sea.

'He's a big baby,' Dr Mullen said. A nurse put him on my chest.

'What time is it?' I asked.

'8.12 p.m.,' the nurse said.

'What's his weight?'

'Nine pounds, six ounces. He's twenty-two inches long.'

The baby lay on my chest and I put a hand protectively on his back. Welcome to the world. Bob took a photograph. I had never felt a greater sense of achievement or contentment.

Nearly five years later, look at me. I began coughing. My eyes felt like two peeled grapes and the skin under my nose was chapped. My sandy hair was brittle and dark-brown and I weighed 8 stone 1 with my boots on. I was way too thin. My bony fingers clutched the white chenille bedspread that I had placed over my duvet for extra warmth. My forehead hurt. I kept coughing – not a gentle, ladylike clearing of the throat kind of cough, but a deep, hacking, foghorn-like bronchial cough, which would have cleared a bus queue or a large section of a cinema. A plague cough. Many years earlier I had attended a discussion of Merce Cunningham's work at Lincoln Center in New York, and a row full of older women with Susan Sontag-style white stripes in their jet-black hair had turned around to glare at me when I coughed like that.

Pat waited patiently for the hacking to subside. 'I had a physical breakdown about ten years ago. The GP gave me so many antibiotics and I got so weak, I thought I was going to die.

That's when I discovered alternative medicine. I had reflexology and started burning lavender. Did you read the Maggie Tisserand book on aromatherapy that I gave you?'

'Yes, I loved it. But Pat, did you know that she wrote the book after divorcing Robert Tisserand, a leading aromatherapist?'

'I had forgotten.'

'That must have taken a lot of lavender.'

I heard a thump and then my son appeared and jumped on the bottom of my brass bed. He had light brown hair with a few blond streaks and large, sombre, brown eyes that immediately conveyed a thoughtful intelligence.

'Mummy, Sally wants me to learn my lines for the Christmas play.'

'OK, darling, just let me finish talking to Pat. Then we can rehearse.'

'I only have one line. I'm a king. I come in after Andrew.'

I put down the receiver and looked at Conor. 'Oh, you're one of the Three Wise Men. Right. What does Andrew say in the play?'

'I bring you gold.'

'Then what do you say?'

'I bring you Frankenstein.'

With that Conor sped out of the room and hurtled triumphantly down the stairs. I heard a thud, then a click, and then the music from *The Lion King* as he put on a video in the living room.

Pat was waiting patiently at the other end of the line, puffing on a cigarette.

'Pat, sorry, I've got to go.'

'Bye for a while, dearie,' she said, hoarsely, 'and give my love to the child.'

At last I hung up and leaned back on the pillow, spent. If I ever get out of this bed, I'm going to do something about the flesh-coloured wallpaper, I thought. I looked at a watercolour hanging on the wall of camels walking past some Moorish buildings. The yellows, greens and browns in the painting soothed me. I had bought it on holiday in January 1995 in Gran Canaria, in a little market stall near the sea. From the stall in Maspalomas I could see the sand dunes of the Sahara Desert, which looked just like the scene in *Lawrence of Arabia* when Peter O'Toole arrives on top of a camel, singing 'I'm the Man Who Broke the Bank at Monte Carlo'.

During that two-week stay in Maspalomas I had taken Conor, then aged three, on a camel ride high in the hills of Gran Canaria. Manolo, the camel-driver, had strapped my young son to my waist.

He gave the adults tea before the ride to calm our nerves. He explained that the camels were muzzled because they might bite. Perhaps the camels should have been given the tea, I remember thinking. But our camel, whose name was Delia, seemed amiable, if a bit mangy. I held on tightly to Conor as we passed under orange trees on rocky hill paths. I felt the heat of the sun on my shoulders and back. A local photographer had snapped our picture and the result was in a brown-and-gold frame on the windowsill beside my sickbed. Looking at the photograph, it was difficult to tell whose legs were skinniest: the camel's, Conor's, or mine.

I looked away from the photograph and the watercolour and out my bedroom window, an act I repeated many times each day. It was another wintry afternoon in south County Dublin, the kind of Irish day that never really gets off the ground. I picked up a brown folder on the bed and glanced at my latest medical report. I read the words 'Epstein Barr virus positive'.

A few weeks earlier my GP had left a message on my answering machine: 'Good news. It's glandular fever.'

'Why is that good news?' I asked in exasperation when I phoned him back.

'Because we thought we might have to remove your gall bladder.'

Glandular fever at age forty? I asked aloud, to no one in particular. Mononucleosis, the 'kissing disease' of college students?

'I wouldn't spread the news around,' my elderly gynaecologist advised when I told him what the GP had said.

'That's *not* how I got it!' I yelled.

He thought for a minute and said, 'It's also milk-borne.'

I recalled buying milk in cartons in Gran Canaria. On reflection it had not been very cold and it had tasted different. The heat of the Saharan sun in the Canary Islands, the Spanish refrigeration, my lousy immune system, who knows? It had never occurred to me to be cautious about milk. I had been so glad to see the sun and feel the dry heat after the winter in Ireland. The cleaning lady had arrived every morning with a smile. '*Hola!*' she'd say to Conor in greeting, and he'd call out to me, 'Mum, Hola's here!'

Wearily I put the medical report back in its folder. My eye caught an advertisement in the community newsletter, lying on top of a pile of half-read newspapers on the floor beside my bed. The ad consisted of an awkward drawing of two feet in a circle. One foot was planted firmly on the ground and the other was inclined slightly in a tapping position. The feet were attached to unusually thick ankles and underneath the big toes were the words 'Stepping to Better Health'. I read on:

> Reflexology. For relief from backache, sciatica, whiplash, sports injuries, arthritis, asthma, sinusitis, stress, migraine, reduced immunity and many other complaints. Contact: Mary Dixon MSRI SRCN 7 days...

The address and phone number had been torn off. I looked at my feet and then I looked again at the ad and wondered if reflexology hurt. I liked the phrase 'reduced immunity'. The ailments in the ad began with capital letters, as though the copywriter had taken them seriously. I liked the quirky drawing of the thick ankles and toes. I tried to focus my mind. Pat had just mentioned the word reflexology when describing her own physical breakdown and recovery.

With effort I pulled the Dublin telephone directory up on to the bed and looked under D for Dixon. There was only one listing for Mary Dixon, with a telephone number beginning 427, an exchange on the north side of Dublin. Why would a northside reflexologist advertise in a southside community newsletter? Would I be strong enough to drive down to the station and get on the DART? I looked at my medical report, I looked at my feet and I looked at the phone. I did not want to lie in this bed for another sixteen weeks, staring at the flesh-coloured wallpaper and taking antibiotics.

Hope lived.

I dialled.

An old man with a deep voice answered the phone on the third ring with a loud 'Hello?'

I'd been living in Ireland long enough to recognise a Donegal accent when I heard one.

'May I speak to Mary Dixon, please?' I asked, wincing. My Boston accent was nasal at the best of times but with glandular fever I sounded like John F. Kennedy with pneumonia.

'Mary Dixon?'

He sounded offended.

Neither of us spoke.

Some time passed and my discomfort grew. The silence became apocalyptic. I was about to murmur an apology for disturbing him when at last the old man, in a voice wracked by grief and rage, roared into the phone: 'Mary Dixon is dead.'

'How bad am I?' I asked a few weeks later.

'You have the worst immune system I've ever worked on,' Mary Dixon said. She knew that the feet do not lie.

'Thank you.'

'Drop your shoulders and relax.'

I leaned back in a big, deep, comfortable armchair in Mary Dixon's reflexology room and folded my hands across my chest, corpse-like. I put my bare feet up on the foot-rest and breathed deeply while she adjusted the cushions beneath my head and elbows. Tea tree oil was burning in an aromatherapy holder in the corner. Phil Coulter's *Sea of Tranquillity* was coming from a tape cassette player on the floor. A plaque on the wall said 'Institute of Reflexologists in Ireland'.

Mary Dixon was a no-nonsense woman in her mid-forties with alert blue eyes and short black hair who lived in Shankill, County Dublin. I tracked her down when the next issue of the community newsletter arrived though the letterbox. This time, when I spotted the ad 'Stepping to Better Health', the phone number was intact. It began with 282, a southside exchange. That's more like it, I thought.

I looked up the word reflexology in my *Pocket Oxford English Dictionary*: 'a system of massage used to relieve tension and treat illness, based on the theory that there are points on the feet, hands and head linked to every part of the body'.

Then I dialled her number.

'I had glandular fever, too,' Mary said.

'You did?'

'When I was studying for my paediatric nursing exams. It flattened me. It's one of the reasons I became a reflexologist.'

'Did you take antibiotics when you had glandular fever?'

'I did, but I haven't taken an antibiotic in eleven years.'

I almost wept with relief.

Mary gave me directions to her home on Hazelwood Drive, around the corner from the house I had been renting since the break-up of my marriage. My son and I lived in the last house in the cul-de-sac, 98A Eaton Wood Grove; it was as though the A in the address stood for Afterthought. It was a detached, comfortable three-bedroom house, about ten years old, with a large back garden that really was a fenced-in field.

'The last lady who lived here was separated, too,' a neighbour said when I moved in.

I landed on Mary Dixon's doorstep, a wan figure in a faded sheepskin jacket, snuffling and shuffling self-consciously, wondering where I was going to remove my nylon stockings and shoes. Mary opened the door, appraised me in a swift, friendly way and showed me into a corner room in her modern redbrick home. She pointed to the door of an adjoining bathroom where I could change, then she tactfully disappeared. I emerged barefoot a few minutes later and entered the reflexology room. Its light blue wallpaper, easy chair and soothing smell of baby powder put me somewhat at ease.

I looked at a book on Mary's desk. The title was *Stories the Feet Can Tell Thru Reflexology/Stories the Feet Have Told Thru Reflexology* by Eunice D. Ingham Stopfel. I picked up the volume and flipped through the book, which contained several diagrams of feet divided into numbered zones. There was a picture of the author looking helpful and serene, her grey hair piled on top of her head. My eye fell on the sentence, 'Transgression against the laws of nature is the root of our afflictions,' and I made a mental note to buy the book.

She began rubbing my toes. Gradually I relaxed and asked her questions about reflexology. Foot massage was practised in ancient Egypt, China and India, she said. In the early twentieth century, Dr William Fitzgerald – a graduate of the University of Vermont, who had spent time at Boston City Hospital, St Francis Hospital, Hartford, Connecticut, and the Central London Nose and Throat Clinic – developed his theory of zone therapy. He believed that an intricate signal system in the feet corresponded to every organ and cell in the body.

'The way I understand it is that the feet are the mirror image of the body,' Mary said.

Eunice D. Ingham Stopfel was a disciple of Dr Fitzgerald and she developed charts and books for what came to be known as reflexology. By the 1990s in Ireland, with the emergence of superbugs resistant to antibiotics, reflexology had started to become a popular alternative therapy for an Irish public increasingly sceptical of GPs and their prescription pads. It was regarded as complementary to, not a replacement for, orthodox medicine. Patients did not appear to be rushing to cancel bypass heart surgery at Blackrock Clinic to attend reflexologists, but anecdotal evidence suggested that more people were finding it helpful for a number of lesser ailments for which orthodox medicine had no cure. Glandular fever was one of these ailments. My GP had told me to eat green vegetables and go to bed for six months. My reflexologist was offering to help boost my immune system with almost immediate effect.

Mary rubbed and kneaded my toes with her hands and I felt relief in the area just above my eyes. 'Your sinuses,' she said.

After rubbing some more, she asked, 'Has someone been painting your house?'

'My God, how did you know that?' I shouted. Tony Wood was painting the kitchen.

'From the reflexes in the tops of your little toes.'

I remained silent.

'Your lower back is in bits,' Mary continued. 'And what have you been doing to your neck and shoulders?'

'Trying to write an outline for a book.'

'Is it fiction?'

'No, creative non-fiction.'

'Creative non-fiction?'

'It's the new fiction.'

'Is there a plot?'

'Not really. I'm not that interested in plot, but the story is based on real events, using novelistic techniques.'

It was true. I wasn't as interested in plot as I was in synchronicity, which my *Oxford Concise English Dictionary* defined as 'the simultaneous occurrence of events which appear significantly related but have no discernible connection', but I was too tired to tell Mary that.

'Who said creative non-fiction is the new fiction?' Mary asked.
'I did.'

Mary rubbed the sides of my little toes. 'What's it about?'

'I'm not going to tell you. You're going to have to read the book.'

'Will you tell me the title?'

'I'm afraid not.' I yawned, coughed, putting a hand over my mouth, then closed my eyes, which, Mary knew, was a signal that I didn't want to speak.

'Did you see the herbalist?'

'Yes.' I mustered enough energy to tell Mary the story of my visit. I had been waiting to see him for some time. He had a long waiting list.

A friend had said to me: 'Glandular fever? Sean Boylan will have a cure.' Brent drove me to his clinic in Dunboyne. Sean was stocky and strong, quick and smart, as you might expect of the manager of the Meath football team. He felt the swollen glands in my neck and under my arms, and looked at me with concern. He gave me herbs from the Himalayas. After taking them for six weeks, I might begin to feel better, he said. He gave me hope and a kiss on the cheek, and wished me well.

Out in the sunny reception area, his assistant handed me two brown bottles, one big and one small. She wore a white lab coat over her jumper and jeans. 'Your herbs,' she said, cheerfully. 'Herbs for energy and herbs for sinus.'

'Which is which?'

'The small bottle contains the herbs for energy. You mix that with boiling water and drink it like tea. The tall bottle is for sinuses. To take these herbs you need to drop your head.'

I didn't understand.

'Pour a dessertspoonful into a small measuring cup and place the herbs in your mouth. Don't swallow them, throw your head back like this instead,' she said, demonstrating. 'Then lean forward and let the herbs drain over your sinuses. Count from one to seven, then slowly swallow them.'

'What are these Himalayan herbs?'

'Chrysanthemum leucanthemum.'

'Chrysanthemum leucanthemum,' I repeated.

I tottered home and placed my battered faith in the power of these herbs. In my kitchen I measured them out like a rocket scientist, pouring the sacred liquids into my damaged immune system with the faith of someone who has few options left. I threw my head back, placed the herbs in my mouth, then leaned forward and counted to seven, letting the herbs slowly trickle down over my sinuses before swallowing. Then I made what I came to call my Himalayan jungle juice. I boiled the kettle, mixed 60 mls of boiled water with 2.5 mls of herbs, let the mixture cool, then drank it like tea. It smelled clean and fresh and tasted like liquid celery.

I repeated this ritual for weeks and months, and slowly and steadily my energy began to return.

The idea of Himalayan herbs called to mind New Zealander Edmund Hillary and Sherpa Tenzing on Mount Everest, and James Hilton's *Lost Horizon* and Shangri-La, the secret valley of eternal youth, where the people lived by the philosophy: 'Here we shall stay with our books and our music and our meditations, conserving the frail elegance of a dying age.' The reality was much more mundane, as I discovered one day, months later, when I rang the clinic to order more herbs.

'You know my Himalayan herbs, the chrysanthemum leucanthemum. What is their English name?'

'Oxi daisies.'

'Excuse me?'

'Oxi daisies, daisies and spring water. And the herb lovage. We call that herb "up the garden". The herbs may have originated in the Himalayas but we grow them here in the back now.'

Daisies and 'up the garden'. Upsy daisy. I groaned, recalling it.

Mary patted me on the left foot, indicating that our session was over. 'Just keep taking the herbs.'

Later that afternoon, when I saw Brent, I asked: 'Do you think I'm doing too much complementary medicine and alternative therapy?'

'Not unless you start bathing yourself in asses' milk,' he replied.

More than two years had passed since I first heard Brent's piano concerto. When I was well enough to work on the project again, we discussed some ideas: what about a soundtrack for an animated film, recorded by a Hungarian orchestra in Hungary?

No.

What about a Dublin concert with an Irish orchestra and a Hungarian piano soloist?

No.

I was working on another proposal and I asked Brent to write a paragraph for me about the concerto. He wrote:

> At first three pieces were written named the 'Three Centuries Suite': nineteenth-century Romantic, twentieth-century Romantic and mock Baroque. Later, reacting to a didactic message from Boulez about the validity of writing anything that isn't modern, a melody was thought of which had no tune, no life, no interest. This became the first theme of the concerto. It represented the authority of the Russian occupiers of Hungary and is opposed by the piano entry, which represents the Hungarian student dissident. So we start. Later the nineteenth-century Romantic piece becomes the lake scene in the first movement; the twentieth-century Romantic piece becomes the beginning of the second movement, which relates to the pianist's childhood; and

the mock Baroque opens the third movement,
representing the campus of a music conservatorium.

Still nothing happened.

The breakthrough came in the spring of 1995. Bobby
Houlihan was coming to Dublin and Brent and I arranged to
meet him for lunch at Dicey Reilly's on Harcourt Street. Dark-
haired, quiet, powerful and self-contained, Bobby arrived carrying
a copy of Beethoven's *Pastoral Symphony* in his briefcase. He had a
plan: he suggested that his Hungarian orchestra perform Brent's
concerto in Dublin with an Irish pianist. He mentioned Finghin
Collins.

A Dublin concert with a Hungarian orchestra and an Irish
pianist?

Yes.

How would we get the Hungarian orchestra to Ireland?

'Talk to the Hungarian ambassador,' Bobby said. 'Send me the
orchestral parts,' he told Brent. Then he turned to me and said,
'You do the blah, blah, blah.'

'Theez eez a breelliant idea whose time has come,' the
Hungarian ambassador to Ireland, Laszlo Mohai, said, as Brent
and I sat before him in the Embassy of the Republic of Hungary
in Fitzwilliam Place, Dublin. It was early 1995. The ambassador
was looking at a copy of our proposal, which I had called 'the
Budapest Project', thinking it sounded vaguely John Le Carré and
Iron Curtain-y.

The idea was to have Brent's piano concerto performed by
a Hungarian orchestra in Ireland on the fortieth anniversary
of the Hungarian Uprising, about eighteen months later. A
commemoration in the National Concert Hall in Dublin would
help to raise Hungary's profile during Ireland's presidency of
the European Union at a time when Hungary was waiting to be
granted membership of the EU.

Bobby already had spoken to Laszlo about sponsorship to

bring his orchestra from Szombatheley to Ireland. Laszlo, a slender, bearded man in his forties, intense and hard-working, with a penchant for delivering wry monologues in a slow, deadpan style, was enthusiastic about the project.

'The Hungarian impostor rang,' said the note in my kitchen one morning soon after. Miriam Darby, the childminder, had left the message. She was a tall, strong nineteen-year-old from Navan who was getting her childcare diploma in Sallynoggin and looking after Conor while I was at work. A smiling girl with long brown hair, she was as warm and steady as the sun. 'Good morning, Mr Magpie,' she would say for luck if she saw only one bird.

Miriam did not mean the Hungarian 'impostor'. I knew who she meant: he phoned frequently. We had entered a crucial period of planning. He had the go-ahead for the Dublin concert, with Brent's concerto as the centrepiece, and it was all systems go, all hands on deck, panic stations, in fact.

The ambassador's plans had mushroomed into an entire week of 'Hungarians in Hibernia' involving film, food, art and the Fire Flower folk-dancers from Paks, who were performing a selection from *Riverdance*. Bobby and the Savaria Symphony Orchestra were undertaking a provincial tour of Ireland, in addition to the big Dublin concert. Father Pat Ahern, founder and artistic director of Siamsa Tíre, was going to host the Hungarian orchestra in Tralee.

I had attended a meeting with Father Pat in Dicey Reilly's and had been puzzled by his involvement; between Siamsa Tíre and the priesthood he was already a busy man. Everyone else had a clear-cut interest: the ambassador wanted his high-profile cultural week; Bobby wanted an Irish tour for his orchestra; Brent and I wanted his *Piano Concerto No 1 in G Major* to be performed in the National Concert Hall. 'What is your interest, Father?' I asked one night on the telephone.

'Didn't you know?'

I waited.

'Bobby grew up in an industrial school in Tralee.'

'Did you know him as a boy in Kerry?'

'Yes.'

Brent sent the orchestral parts to Hungary. One day there was a knock on the door of his music room in Adelaide Road. Finghin Collins had come round to collect the piano score of Brent's concerto. Things were moving now.

The 'Hungarians in Hibernia' festival week was an extremely ambitious proposal but the ambassador was willing to take on all the responsibility himself, despite the fact that he was not an impresario. Power shifted from the original organising committee, comprising a New Zealand composer, an Irish-American journalist, an Irish conductor living in France and a Kerry priest, to the ambassador and the Hungarian government.

I still did the blah, blah, blah. I kept everyone aware of what was happening and tried to ensure that the original concept of the Dublin concert was retained. There were difficulties. Laszlo would not allow any publicity about the concert until it was almost too late. Having spent most of his life under communism, he was unaccustomed to the concept of an independent media, to put it mildly. It was a cultural difference and it was frustrating. A free press seemed to make him nervous, so he allowed very little information to be released to the papers leading up to the festivities. How were people supposed to know that the concert was on? Sponsors were lined up. Egos soared. Ambassadorial nerves jangled. Journalistic tempers flared. Tickets went on sale. Fliers were produced. Music critics were grinding their teeth.

Brent remained calm. The arrangements twisted and turned, and as more and more people got into the act the concert began to evolve from our initial idea. At some stages I thought the Budapest Project would go off the rails. I warned Brent that there were problems; there were other interests. The concerto might not go on. 'The die is cast,' Brent said.

'The hell it is,' I said.

After a few heated phone calls and one or two four-letter words, the programme was finalised. The piano concerto was to be performed. The big day, 27 October 1996, was approaching – the Sunday of the bank holiday weekend – and I was having trouble getting a childminder.

Bobby's Hungarian orchestra arrived in Ireland on a flight arranged by the ambassador. The idea that a sixty-piece orchestra was going to be flown from provincial Hungary to Dublin had a dreamlike quality until the morning of the orchestral rehearsal when I stepped on to the choir balcony of the National Concert Hall and looked down at the stage. A hazel-eyed Hungarian holding a cello smiled up at me. They were here.

The musicians – thirty men and thirty women – had worn casual clothes during the morning rehearsal, but on the night of the concert their black evening attire sparkled and their hair shone. The 1,200-seat concert hall was packed and buzzing. The long gleaming Steinway grand piano was wheeled on to the stage and out came Finghin Collins, tawny-haired and all of nineteen years old.

Brent's concerto began. As he played, Finghin looked like a beautiful horse running through a field. The Hungarian orchestra was immaculate and Bobby was conducting at break-neck speed, which added to the excitement. Twenty-two minutes later the work was over and the audience erupted. Bobby signalled for the composer to come up to the stage. The applause was tumultuous.

As Brent climbed the steps, a section of the audience in front of me in the National Concert Hall let out a roar, the kind of roar that you hear at Old Trafford when Manchester United score a goal against Chelsea. Brent bowed deeply to the Hungarian musicians and then to the audience.

I watched with deep satisfaction. I loved the piano concerto, and I loved the composer of the work even more.

The orchestra performed many encores and Strauss waltzes,

and Bobby was enjoying himself so much that he appeared reluctant to leave the stage.

At the end of the concert Laszlo spoke. Mindful of Ireland's role as president of the EU and of its help to Hungary in the past, he said: 'Forty years ago we made a desperate attempt to return to the place we had held for centuries in the family of the European nations.' After the 1956 uprising had been crushed, forcing many Hungarians to seek shelter in Western countries, 'Ireland was one of those who offered help and home for the hopeless Hungarians. We will never forget that.'

Afterwards the Hungarian ambassador, who had become my friend during the long, tumultuous months of planning, turned to me and said: 'Thank you. You did what you said you would do.'

7

LETTER FROM NORMAN

'Return to Castlebar,' I said to the young man behind the counter at Heuston Station. He wore a crimson V-neck sweater with 'Iarnród Éireann' on the crest. It was April 1998.

'Coming back today?'

'No, in three days.'

'£22.'

After handing him the cash I headed straight for the newsagent. 'Ladies and gentleman,' the announcer said, 'the train now standing at platform four is the 8.05 to Westport.' It was cold in the station at 7.45 a.m. I bought newspapers in one shop, tea in another and walked to platform four. I stopped to have my ticket checked, then boarded the mud-spattered orange-and-black train.

I walked through the first couple of carriages. In the first I found an old man reading *The Irish Times* with a magnifying glass. In the second I met a group of nuns on their way to the shrine at Knock. They wore civilian clothes with silver crosses around their necks and were darting back and forth in unexpected movements, like a gaggle of hungry geese. In the third carriage, I chose an empty group of four seats with a table where I could spread out my newspapers and remove the cover of my takeaway tea.

The train guard announced: 'Ladies and gentlemen, this is the 8.05 train to Westport, serving Newbridge, Kildare, Portarlington, Tullamore, Clara, Athlone, Roscommon, Castlerea, Ballyhaunis,

Claremorris, Manulla Junction and Castlebar. Change at Manulla Junction for Foxford and Ballina.'

The train rumbled off and I opened the *Guardian*. I looked up once during the first thirty minutes and saw three people on horseback on the Curragh. The next half-hour was uneventful, and when I looked up again we were passing a traveller halting-site in Tullamore. 'Ladies and gentleman, the train is now arriving in Athlone. Athlone is our next stop. Passengers change for Galway at Athlone.'

Athlone station was busy. Conductors and Network Catering staff boarded the train and the atmosphere on board became slightly more official. The veneer of authority was quickly dispelled, however, when an old woman sat down across the aisle from me and put her feet up on the seat opposite, sturdy black shoes and all. The morning sun warmed the carriage. After several minutes she took off her coat and settled back to read the *Mayo News*. A group of schoolboys, supervised by two fit young men in bright fleeces, boarded the train.

'Please stand clear of all doors. The doors will close.' The train pulled away from the station. Within minutes I saw a great green dome, a mart, a platform, a green fence and a series of semi-detached houses. We were approaching the River Shannon. As we crossed the river, I could see the Athlone boat club to the left. A few boats bobbed serenely to my right and a pair of swans glided alongside one of the cruisers. I looked at the big sky. I felt my shoulders relax as they did when my parents used to drive across the Sagamore Bridge over the Cape Cod Canal when I was a child.

The change of landscape and the sight of the calm river brought such relief. It was the high point of the journey so far.

The train moved on through low-lying Roscommon. I saw fields under water and cows standing in mud. A girl in her First Communion dress stood in a conservatory at the side of a house near the railway line, unaware that she was being admired from the passing train. I could see newborn lambs. The sun was stronger now on the fields. I saw horses, cows, a hare, trees, a farm building, a lake, fences, gorse, power lines, rolling green fields and lots of sheep. Here was the opportunity for bog-watching.

Around eleven I decided to go to the dining car for a cup of tea. I made my way down the aisle, swaying and holding on to the tops of empty seats. The next carriage contained a lone passenger: an imposing white-haired man in a green Barbour rain jacket who looked like Ernest Hemingway without the death wish. He was reading *The Way That I Went* by Robert Lloyd Praeger. As he read, the train bounced and wobbled and sang on the rails.

Before you could say Rabelaisian, I had entered the strange half-light of the smokers' car, the last refuge of the defiantly unhealthy, a place where it was always night. Men and women sat smoking and drinking, with their arms and legs sprawled in the aisle. Two women held cigarettes with the ashes dangling while their toddlers ran back and forth. A man with bloodshot eyes and a scar on his face wore a pair of wraparound sunglasses. Someone coughed uncontrollably. Everyone appeared to be dressed in black. It looked as though the cemeteries had burst, the graves had opened and the dead had walked to the train for a day out.

I trudged on until I reached the dining car, where a young man with a shaved head, wearing a short-sleeved white shirt and black trousers, eyed me ruefully. I ordered a cup of tea, paid £1 for a half-filled plastic container that was too hot to hold in my hand, and made my way back to my seat, battle-weary. We were approaching the Mayo border.

At times the train seemed to stop more than it started. Maddeningly, it halted for long periods and for no apparent reason. At Ballyhaunis I heard noises reminiscent of creaking metal, like the sinking of the *Titanic*. 'We'd like to apologise for the delay due to engineering works on the line,' the conductor announced with old-world courtesy.

'It'd be faster if I got out and pushed it,' a middle-aged man said on his mobile phone.

The trip was becoming more than tedious and I was beginning to feel trapped. I thought of my father singing 'Passengers will please refrain/From flushing toilets/While the train is standing in the station/I love you' while we were caught in long tailbacks on Route 3 from Cape Cod to Boston.

At last the train lurched forward and we continued our journey. 'Passengers at the rear of the train, please move forward in order to reach the platform safely. Claremorris is our next stop. Would they please move up so that they can reach the platform on arrival.' Whoooooosh went the train.

At Claremorris station a young woman in her early twenties with pale-blue eyes and shoulder-length blond hair boarded. She read a thick textbook as we rolled through the Mayo countryside.

I got my first glimpse of Croagh Patrick after Manulla Junction, and my heart quickened at the sight of the Reek. I could see the path beaten up the side of St Patrick's mountain by thousands of pilgrims over the centuries. On the right was the Nephin range. Next stop was Castlebar. I looked at my watch: 11.40. Within ten minutes I saw hanging baskets with flowers and a sign at the station that said *Fáilte go Caisleán an Bharraigh*, Welcome to Castlebar, from the Castle of the Barrys.

I arrived, blinking at freedom, needing to stretch my legs after four hours on the train. I stood in the sunshine, appreciating the stillness of the west of Ireland after the din of Dublin city-centre. My destination was Achill Island – only thirty-eight miles to go.

Seven years earlier, when my son was a baby, I had spent a week's holiday on Achill. As I sat outside in the September sunshine, I noticed a house across the road, set way back under the Minaun Cliffs, and an older man, wearing dark reading glasses and bright summer clothes, walking down a driveway behind some sheep.

I wondered about the faraway house and the approaching man, who had a studious air. Were they his sheep? Hardly. He may have been an individualist but he wasn't a rugged individualist, the kind of person you expected to find in Achill's elemental landscape. He was incongruous in this terrain. He didn't look like the black-haired man with the strong build who had rumbled past on the blue tractor. He looked like Jean-Paul Sartre going to the beach.

When he reached the bottom of the driveway, the sheep turned towards the sea and the man turned right, in my direction. They aren't his sheep, I concluded. Oh no, I thought, as I sat alone beside twelve-week-old Conor, asleep in his pram. Jean-Paul Sartre is heading straight for me.

My visitor introduced himself as Norman Hudis, an English screenwriter who lived in Woodland Hills, in the San Fernando Valley of California. Born in 1922 in London, in the heart of the east end, he was sixty-nine when we met. He exuded a life of the mind but he had a lighter side too. He had written the first six *Carry On* movies forty years before, and had bought the house on the hill, 'a wild gift', as he called it, for his Irish wife Rita, inspiration for *Carry on Nurse*. He wrote the movie after spending ten days in a British hospital following an appendectomy.

We sat in the sun and chatted. He had watched my arrival from the cottage on the hill, and he and Rita had been amused by the amount of baby paraphernalia I had packed on top of the car and my endless trips into the rented cottage to set up the equipment.

I had been visiting Irish islands for more than a dozen years. Since my Watson Fellowship days, I had been clambering on board trawlers or sailboats to visit islands off the west coast of Ireland, especially Inishbofin, whenever I could, free and easy, wearing my Wellingtons and tossing my luggage on to the shore. After my father died in 1981, I took unpaid leave from my job as a reporter and spent a month on 'Bofin, working for Margaret Day in the hotel and walking off my grief. John Behan was staying in Day's with his children and I enjoyed his company. His sculpture of the legend of the white cow was hanging on the wall of the hotel. I remember him reading Henry Miller at breakfast in Day's and getting straight to work afterwards. I liked his simplicity, his sensitivity and his Dublin decency; when he shook hands in greeting, I noticed his right hand was as strong as a rock. I laughed when he told me about someone who had written a novel about Steak Diane. Slowly I was recovering from my father's death. One day when I was on a break, sitting in the sunshine, John drew a quick sketch of me, which I have to this day.

After a month or so on the island, when most of the visitors had gone, I realised it was time to get back to work. I rang the *New York Daily News* from a phone booth on 'Bofin and got Sam Roberts, the city editor. 'Where are you?' he asked.

'Inishbofin, the island of the white cow.'

'How's the weather?'

'Gorgeous.'

'Take me with you.'

'Sam, I want to come back to work.'

'Great. You're going nights in Manhattan.' He hung up.

Paddy O'Halloran, the skipper, stood with me on the old pier as I was getting ready to leave, watching a pair of beautiful horses.

'They say the dog is most like the human,' Paddy said to me, 'but I say it's the horse.'

In 1991, with the arrival of the baby and all the gear of modern parenting, I had to find another way to get to my islands. Basically I needed an island I could drive to, and Achill, connected to the mainland by a bridge at Achill Sound, was the answer. It is Ireland's largest offshore island: beautiful, powerful, with a population of almost 3,000, and accessible. I called it Inishbofin for beginners.

As we sat in the sunshine in Dookinella, on what felt like the last road in the west, I told Norman a bit of my story and he told me his. Rita's mother, Ethel Marjory McDowell, had been born in McDowell's Hotel on the Slievemore Road, Achill. Apparently one of Rita's forebears was one of the early Protestants on the island. He was a deserter from the British army in the 1800s and swam across Achill Sound with a Bible strapped around his waist, arriving on the island with little else, as Norman put it, but the Good Book. That was the extent of Norman's link to Achill and he found the west of Ireland a difficult place. He faxed his scripts to various producers and agents, went for walks on the beach and listened to Wagner's *Ring* cycle during harsh winter gales.

Rita loved the island way of life and so did I. After years of working for news organisations in New York and Dublin, I relished it, but Norman's loneliness was evident. I mentioned that my maternity leave was ending and in a few days I had to return to Dublin, where I worked as a journalist. 'I wish I could throw a net over you,' he said mournfully.

Norman, urban and urbane, longed for the cinemas, sidewalks and traffic lights of Los Angeles, six thousand miles away. He must have been close to breaking point with rural living when we met. He was finishing a script and he had run out of fax paper, which meant driving to Westport to replenish his supply. I wondered if his seaweed-gathering days in Achill were numbered.

For a bit of light relief, he invited me up to see his house, which, from a distance, looked like a lighthouse-keeper's cottage on the moon. 'Remarkable,' I said, standing at the top of his driveway. It was a magnificent day and the sun was a shock and a relief after the grey skies of Dublin. The property had an unobstructed view of the sea and three miles of sandy beach at Keel. Standing near a bank of montbretia with vivid red and orange blossoms, I took in Minaun, Croaghaun and Slievemore mountains. Starlings sat on the telephone wire; smoke billowed from a chimney. On the side of the cliffs I saw a white-haired man in a red cap directing sheep dogs, waving a walking stick as though he was conducting a symphony.

We found Rita barbecuing in the back, out of the wind. She let me peek inside the house. It was rustic but comfortable, with large picture windows in every room. What would it be like to live there? I imagined that, with the light changing on the mountains and the panoramic sea views, it would be like waking up in an art gallery.

Conor and I had arrived in Dookinella, from the Irish *Dumhach Cionn Aille*, 'sand dune at the end of the cliff', the day before. The weather was bright and clear. We crossed the Michael Davitt Bridge and drove through Cashel and Bunnacurry. We came to the top of a hill where we met such a heart-stopping view of sky, mountains, sea and bog that I pulled over to the side of the road to take it in. I stepped out of the car into a strong breeze. You could drink the air. Mountains surrounded the bay. A woman in an old red car drove slowly behind two cows, one tawny and the other brown. Whitewashed cottages nestled peacefully on either side of the road.

I drove down the hill, slowing as I came to a crossroads. A sign on the right-hand side of the road with the words 'Fr Sweeney Memorial' pointed towards the shore. The Crossroads Inn stood on the far left corner. I turned left and drove down a road which was long and winding, with potholes in places. A group of black-and-white sheepdogs ran straight for the car, chasing the wheels like the Furies and barking furiously. I slammed on the brakes and rolled up the window on the driver's side. I drove on slowly with the dogs chasing the tyres until I reached a small bridge. The dogs of Dookinella all turned back, as if on cue, and sat down in the middle of the road in front of a two-storey yellow house.

A primary school was sitting serenely above the road on the left-hand side. Three horses were standing in a field in front of a disused, flat-roofed house to the right. I stopped the car again as a hen crossed the road; it appeared to be wearing a hat. It had something, a piece of paper or cloth, covering its ear. Oh to be in Dookinella, where men are men and the hens wear hats. I drove on until I got a glimpse of the cliffs and stopped in front of a small house, set close to the road, which I had rented from a Bord Fáilte guide. I parked the car, got out, and took a good look around. The fencing was crude, made with posts and wire and repaired with bits of timber and rope. More than one hundred and fifty years after the Great Hunger it was still a Famine landscape, barren and hard-scrabble. In the mid-nineteenth century, before the bridge, life couldn't have got much harder than it had been on this road, but today it was more the memory of hardship. I watched an older man in a wetsuit walk towards the sea with a surfboard under his arm. There was an untrammelled beauty, a freedom and contentment at the end of this seaside road.

Out of this terrain emerged my new friend Norman. After my holiday ended we kept in touch. In the early 1990s, before e-mail, this meant writing letters, which took a week to cross the ocean between Dublin and Los Angeles. He wrote single-spaced letters on an electric typewriter, and I wrote back to him on my old Amstrad word processor. Our pattern of occasional correspondence continued for years.

I recall his protest when the Pope appeared to abolish hell as a literal place. Norman, who is Jewish, was sympathetic to the confusion and hurt of Catholics who suddenly had been told to disregard thousands of years of teaching. Norman sent me a clipping from the *Los Angeles Times* about an editorial, approved by the Vatican, which appeared in the Jesuit journal *La Civiltà Cattolica*. The editorial said: 'Hell exists, not as a place but as a state, a way of being of the person who suffers the pain of the deprivation of God.' Norman wrote to me:

> For twenty centuries, the official church has frightened children – and adults – into nightmares over the existence of a physical and geographical hell, where unendurable penalties are inflicted on a scale and with a ferocious assiduity infinitely worse than anything Stalin or Hitler dreamed up. Now, on the sudden infallible say-so of the present Pope, this is all dismissed as a misconception.

The Pope's thoughts on hell came a week after his discourse on heaven, which, he said, is 'neither an abstraction nor a physical place in the clouds, but a living and personal relationship of union with the Holy Trinity.'

Norman wrote: 'Without offence to anyone who holds genuine and simple Christian beliefs, I am very curious to know how this truly extraordinary turnabout has struck people who have been brought up, for generations, to believe exactly the opposite.'

Right on, Norman. It was confusing. As Patsy McGarry, Religious Affairs Correspondent of *The Irish Times*, observed, 'Hell is now a state of mind – like New York.'

I, in turn, sent Norman despairing dispatches from Celtic Tiger Dublin, where newfound prosperity was beginning to wreak havoc: 'Dear Norman, Everyone in Dublin is driving around in company cars on EU-built roads, talking on mobile phones and knocking each other down. This is not why I left New York.'

Dublin was changing, getting richer, faster and more unmanageable. When I left *The Irish Times* office at night after work in the 1980s, the city was virtually deserted and the night sky was filled with smoke from bituminous coal in people's fireplaces. In the 1990s I noticed that the city-centre was as busy at night as it had been during the day. If I worked late, the security guards would be horrified that I intended to walk alone to my car in the car-park in Temple Bar and would offer to accompany me. This safety-consciousness was new in my Irish experience. When I joined the paper in 1987, a German tourist was killed in the Phoenix Park and it was shocking, page one news. In the Ireland I came to, there were crimes against property, but not so many against the person. Murders were becoming commonplace in 1990s Ireland. Public order offences and raucous behaviour were making the city-centre as unpleasant as any bad section of an American city.

In January 1998, Norman wrote and said that Rita's mother had died and that he and Rita were thinking of selling their house in Achill. 'Do you know anybody who would like to buy our house?' he asked in the letter.

I had been pretty low. On 17 December 1997, eight days before Christmas, I had obtained an Irish divorce, one of the first few hundred in the State since the passage of the divorce referendum in 1996. The court proceedings had been as dignified as they had been painful. Judge Elizabeth Dunne was kind when I took the stand to answer questions about where the marriage had taken place and how long we had been apart. My answers would lead to the undoing of the vows pledged so earnestly in Our Lady of Grace Church fourteen years earlier.

I phoned Norman in Los Angeles about the house. 'What about me?' Norman and Rita made approving noises. They usually got on two extensions when I phoned them, as parents do.

A few weeks later I drove to Achill to stay in the house overnight. I stood in the living room and looked at the sea. The sensation was overwhelming; it was like being on a boat. I went outside with the surveyor. 'Grab it,' he said, his measuring tape blowing in the wind. The deeds were immaculate, the solicitors for vendor and purchaser impeccable. And so I did.

House purchases in rural Ireland could be lengthy and complex. A colleague told me that he had been trying to sort out the deeds to an Achill site for forty years and finally had given up. The speed and ease with which my house purchase went through – in a matter of weeks, not months – was striking. It felt as though I had inherited it. In the house Norman left me his classical music tapes, his Oxford English Dictionary and his electric typewriter.

'I never thought you would get it,' the surveyor said.

The more time I spent in the house in Dookinella, the happier and healthier I felt and the more I wanted to live in Achill. The month of May was splendid. The amount of time Conor and I spent outdoors reminded me of my childhood on Cape Cod.

My parents had bought a summer house on Depot Street in Dennisport when I was three or four; at that age I thought that Monomoy Island, which you could see from the beach, was France. We spent every summer on the Cape and most weekends in the spring and autumn. It was a life spent outdoors playing basketball, riding bicycles and swimming in the warm waters of Nantucket Sound. They were happy days, healthy times, reading Louisa May Alcott, J. D. Salinger and, later, Kurt Vonnegut on the beach. Sunny day followed sunny day: there was more swimming and more reading; sometimes we went over to the regional high school and played basketball in the midday heat, then threw ourselves fully clothed into a nearby pond.

The world kept turning as I walked through the living room on my way to and from the beach, the bicycle and the basketball court. There were the quixotic Democratic presidential campaigns by candidates who were opposed to the Vietnam War. Eugene McCarthy, 'Clean Gene', the poetry-writing senator from Minnesota, sought and failed to get the Democratic nomination. McCarthy's campaign was known as the Children's Crusade because so many people who campaigned for him, including myself, were not old enough to vote. Four years later, Senator George McGovern from South Dakota managed to get the Democratic nomination, but lost to Richard Nixon in a landslide. Only Massachusetts and Washington DC's electoral votes went to McGovern.

On Cape Cod the sun rose and set on the landmarks of my childhood and teenage years: Vietnam and the growing anti-war protests, the moon landing, Gloria Steinem and the women's liberation movement, Woodward and Bernstein and Watergate. A family friend, Jimmy Mullins, sent us a photo of himself aboard a small river boat in the Mekong Delta. *Ms* magazine was published. There were peace marches on Washington.

One day in July 1969, when I was thirteen, my father pointed to a grainy image on the television screen. 'Look,' he said.

Neil Armstrong was walking on the moon.

'Houston, Tranquility Base here. The Eagle has landed.'

Then the Apollo 11 astronaut uttered the famous line: 'That's one small step for man, one giant leap for mankind.' He went on to say more, as was noted in *A Patriot's Handbook*, introduced and selected by Caroline Kennedy, JFK's daughter:

> *Armstrong*: The surface is fine and powdery. I can pick it up loosely with my toe. It does adhere in fine layers like powdered charcoal to the sole and the sides of my boots. I only go in a small fraction of an inch, maybe an eighth of an inch, but I can see the footprints of my boots and the treads in the fine sandy particles…
>
> *Houston*: Oh, that looks beautiful from here, Neil.
>
> *Armstrong*: It has a stark beauty all its own. It's like much of the high desert of the United States. It's different but it's very pretty out here…

As someone who hadn't ventured beyond Washington DC yet, I paused to marvel at the risk Neil Armstrong was taking on the moon. I watched the television coverage for a while but the beautiful sunny Cape Cod day was even more compelling. There would have been some discussion in my home about the wisdom of NASA spending all that money in outer space when there were people living in poverty on planet Earth. I jumped on my bicycle and went back to the beach.

I wanted that sense of place and love of the outdoors for Conor and we weren't getting anything remotely like that. My son and I would never have the chance to 'live in the landscape', as John Behan called it, if we stayed in an increasingly congested and overdeveloped south Dublin suburb. I took him to the Cape for a month almost every summer, but that wasn't enough. I wanted a new life for him, but I didn't want to leave Ireland and I didn't want to sever my connection with *The Irish Times*. 'Could we live in the Achill house all year round?' I asked the surveyor.

'That's what it was built for.'

I visited the school. The master would put Conor on the roll. I checked the train schedules from Castlebar to Dublin and timed the drive to the train: one hour. There was one major hitch: my job as a sub-editor in the newsroom of *The Irish Times* was two hundred miles away. Carry On Commuter.

Unbeknownst to me, Fergus Brogan, a colleague who had been living in Kinvarra, County Galway, was in need of a job-share partner. Job-sharing meant slicing your income and pension contributions in half, but it was a progressive option for the parents of young children or journalists who wanted to write or pursue other interests. On the night of the Good Friday agreement, he sent out a message on the internal messaging system at *The Irish Times*: Job-share partner wanted. Non-smoker, he joked. I stared at the message. Could this really be happening? It would free me from having to be in Dublin all the time.

Management kicked around the idea for a while. Staffing numbers were always a contentious issue, but there had been job-sharing precedents. After weeks and months, a managing editor and the chief sub-editor gave consent for me to share my job in the newsroom, and the head of human resources signed the contract. I was free to live in Achill. The idea was that I would travel up on the train, do my two nights' work and then head west the following morning. Some of my colleagues seemed fascinated by the idea and watched with curiosity as I came in and out of the office each week with my bags over my shoulder. 'You've set my brain on fire,' one said.

There was more. Back at the College of Music, Brent was coming up to retirement in June 1998. In July of that year he came to live with Conor and me in Achill after a lifetime in Bray. He moved to an island he had never visited and to a house he had never seen. He videotaped his own arrival and then wrote music to accompany the footage. He filmed the sunsets over Croghaun. He painted the outside of the house while printing out his compositions. He invented a system of composing on computer and then wrote an *Achill Suite*. He produced a torrent of music, including 'Granuaile' and 'Lifeboats'.

I related everything that was happening to a writer friend who was a storyline editor. She said that if she submitted the details of my life in a script, it would be rejected as implausible. 'If this isn't synchronicity, then I don't know what is,' she said.

Conor was then seven, and the move from Castle Park School in Dalkey was going to be a shock. He had been popular there, and Joan, with whom I shared school runs, had been like an aunt. His teachers found him cheerful and pleasant. He was a good soccer player. But with Bob in the States or in hospital in Dublin on his return, and me working full-time at the paper, which meant three evenings per week from 3.45 p.m. until 10.45 p.m. and one night a week from 8.30 p.m. until 3 a.m. on the foreign desk, the stress of my daily life was substantial. I wasn't seeing Conor four nights out of seven. I was near breaking point one day when he was in first class and his teacher told me that he was a bit behind in his reading. 'The Hungarians will be playing your piano concerto and my son won't know how to read,' I snapped at Brent. Incensed that a child of mine would be behind in the area in which I made my living, I spent the next few weeks working with him a bit each morning before we drove over Killiney Hill to pick up Joan's two boys, Nicky and Alex, on our way to school.

'I have something to show you and it's very exciting,' Conor said a few weeks later when I went to collect him from school. His hair was flaxen from playing in the sun during a rare heatwave. I laughed at his precociousness. And then he pulled something out of his schoolbag. It was a trophy from Castle Park, the Silver Cup, presented that morning to Conor at assembly 'for improved reading'. He won the PTA prize for progress later that year as well.

The primary school down the road in Dookinella was a different kettle of fish. The master was articulate and proud and the academic standards were rigorous, but Castle Park's large building and grounds, hot lunches, international student body and morning assemblies with classical music were gone.

'Achill is our amenity now,' I said. The island would have to provide the facilities for extracurricular activities, and it did. The school organised swimming lessons in Westport and computer classes in Crumpawn; we found a piano teacher in the Valley. I bought Conor a wetsuit and surfboard so that he could try surfing on Keel beach. He learned to play Gaelic football with the Dookinella team, a group of determined and hardy footballers who provided a lot of excitement over the years. I went in search of a pair of boots for him; I knew nothing about the game. I waited for the master to arrive at school one morning and got out of my car. 'Are these the right ones?' I asked anxiously, producing a new pair for his inspection. He looked startled: I don't think anyone had asked him that question in forty years.

It was the sport that saved us. Dookinella is a village of small farms and fields scattered along the side of the Minaun Cliffs and the sea side of the road. Almost everybody is related to everybody else and land rarely passed on to strangers, except for holiday home owners who managed to buy sites over the years. At first we had little in common with people on the road except to return their greeting of a long, slow, rural wave. Sport changed that. They needed Conor for the team.

'Guess what?' Conor would say when he got in the car. 'There's training today.'

'Training,' the lads would shout as they ran from school. We'd race home so that he could change and head straight for the Sandybanks, beside the sea in Keel. Brent made a goal out of posts and orange fishnet behind the house and Conor spent hours kicking a ball and practising. We spent several afternoons or evenings a week driving him to training sessions on beautiful, windswept pitches on the Sandybanks beside the golf course or to matches on the newly-developed Michael Davitt pitch beside the secondary school, Scoil Damhnait, in Achill Sound.

'Over the bar, Conor!' I shouted with the other parents.

'Get up, Pádraig!' one mother cried.

'Eddie, get into the game!' another called.

Nothing could have prepared me for the excitement, the community support, the almost life-and-death intensity of Gaelic football matches among primary school children in the west of Ireland. The West Mayo football final, in which the combined Dookinella-Valley-Dooniver team competed, was the most exciting sporting event I have attended in my life. Conor blocked a ball with gloved hands and the crowd in Kilmeena went 'Whooaah'. My heart was pounding. DVD won the West Mayo final and the coach said to me: 'It doesn't get better than this.'

The Irish language proved a challenge. Conor had to give his news each morning in Irish, and the *Nuacht* was making him tense. I didn't have the language and felt helpless; it was Ellis Island in reverse. I phoned a friend who was a fluent Irish-speaker and said, 'I need a verb to get him going.'

'*Chuaigh mé*,' she said.

'What does it mean?'

'I went.'

Many of Conor's sentences began with '*Chuaigh mé*' for a time until he acquired a few more verbs. '*Chuaigh mé go dtí an siopa*,' he said. I went to the shop. And he taught me what to say when he wanted to be excused. '*An bhfuil cead agam dul amach?*' he would ask.

'*Tá*,' I would say proudly, feeling like someone who had just passed their first test at the immigration office.

Brent was thriving up in his composing room. One day he got a phone call from Mayo County Council, which he thought was an answer to a query about refuse charges and the sticker on his wheelie bin. Instead it was Sean Walsh, assistant arts officer, asking him to play a concert of his own music in St Thomas's Church, Dugort, the nineteenth-century chapel built by the evangelical Protestant minister Edward Nangle. The county council rented a Steinway grand for him and the *Irish Independent* covered the arrival of the piano in Achill, with photograph by Ken Wright and report by Tom Shiel:

> Workmen hack out path as prelude to an evening of beautiful music
>
> When Henry Engelhard Steinway built the first of his world's finest pianos 150 years ago, he could hardly have imagined that one day men with saws and hatchets would have to clear a path for one of his stunning creations to be carried though summer foliage to a tiny chapel in the west of Ireland.
>
> That is exactly what local workmen on Achill Island were doing earlier this week in preparation for the arrival at St Thomas's Church, Dugort, of a Steinway grand piano for a performance tonight by New Zealand-born composer Brent Parker.
>
> So constricted had the passage in the historic chapel become that branches had to be lopped and pruned before the huge Steinway could be brought down the driveway to the church door.
>
> Many of the works performed by Brent Parker tonight were written by him in Achill. 'I find the landscape and the sometimes tempestuous sea totally inspirational,' the composer revealed during a break in rehearsals yesterday.

I had the right football boots for Conor and the right composing environment for Brent. For the next six years, I lived a bicoastal existence, travelling between Dookinella and D'Olier Street on the train.

8

FOLLOW THE MOON

'Where's the house?' the delivery man asked.

'Take the Dookinella road towards the Minaun Cliffs,' I said. 'It's the last house on the left before the sea.'

'That's a bad road.'

'It is.'

'Is it the new one near the road?'

'No. It is the last house on the left before the sea.'

Silence from the delivery man.

'If you go too far,' I added, 'turn around on the coast road and come back.'

'Is it beside Mikey Dan?'

'No.'

'Does it have a green roof?'

'No. My house is the last one on the left before the sea. I don't know how else to say it. Blue gate. Brown roof. The house on the hill. Way up the driveway, before the Cathedral Cliffs, on the left-hand side of the road.'

'Are you from America?'

'Yes.'

'What part?'

'Boston.'

More silence from the delivery man. He hadn't been listening to a word I had said.

If he had been delivering the goods at night-time, the

directions to my house in Achill would have been much easier. At night I could have told him simply to follow the moon.

Shortly after we arrived in Mayo I met an old woman with a deep limp, who was walking down the Dookinella road. Holding her cane in front of her, she looked as though she was pulling a gondola. She was small, with intelligent blue eyes, and her face was as weathered as a Maori. She appeared to be in her eighties. A sheepdog followed her, jumping and barking.

'Dirty, filthy, rotten sun,' she muttered through clenched teeth.

I waited as she approached.

Then she said louder: 'Dirty, filthy, rotten sun.' She put her hand over her eyes to shield her face from the dirty, filthy, rotten sun and peered at me. 'You're the lady on the hill.'

'Yes,' I said.

'That's *Áitín Aoibhinn*,' she said, pointing to my property.

'What does it mean?'

'Happy placeen.'

I wanted to ask her how to spell it but refrained.

She turned around to look at Slievemore.

'And that's Slievemore,' I said.

'No,' the old woman said. 'That is my sleeve,' she said, patting the sleeve of her dress. Then she gestured towards the mountain. 'That is Schleeve-more.'

'Schleeve-more,' I repeated.

A tractor rumbled towards us and the old woman began to move down the road.

'You're lucky up on the hill,' she murmured as she was leaving. 'You have the moon.' And with that, she was on her way, throwing a bit of turf at the back of the barking sheepdog. Her throw was surprisingly strong, and when a sod landed with a thump in the middle of his back, the dog yelped.

As we adjusted to living in the house on the hill we began to understand what the old woman meant. The moon would climb over Minaun and rise up over the graves known as *Páistí*

Marbha, on the edge of the sea, where stillborn and unbaptised babies were buried up to the 1950s. Then it would linger on the *cillín* and shine down on our house, right into our living room and kitchen. Eventually it would come to rest over the sea, lighting up Keel Island, where they send the bold sheep. The effect of the moonlight on our house and the surrounding fields in the middle of the night was eerily beautiful and surreal, as though a film director had erected a giant floodlight on the property.

I began to take an interest in *Páistí Marbha* and felt hurt when, during the daytime, I saw hill-walkers stomping on an infants' burial ground without realising what they were doing. Neighbours told me that a baby who was stillborn or who died shortly after birth was taken from the mother and buried in a nearby field, sometimes in a shoe-box, often in the middle of the night in an atmosphere of secrecy, without a headstone or cross to mark the site. This stark ritual developed as a result of the Catholic Church's cruel policy, since abandoned, of refusing to allow unbaptised babies to be buried in consecrated ground. Bereaved family members grieved in silence. It was a sensitive thing, very private, a sad affair, a neighbour told me. People didn't usually talk about it at all.

In the year 2000 there was a move, initiated by the Catholic Church as part of its millennium commemorations with the strong support of local people, to restore the *cillín* in Dookinella, and to have the graves there and in twenty-one other sites on the island blessed. It was hoped that the action would go some way towards healing the pain and hurt caused by the Church.

'There will be a meeting in Dookinella school about the graves known as *Páistí Marbha*,' a notice in the parish newsletter stated one Sunday morning.

'I'm going to that meeting,' I told Brent.

From the small window in my upstairs office I looked at the infants' unmarked graves, which were eroding, and felt a low, burning anger.

The meeting in the primary school was attended by many local people, some of whom had family members in the *cillín*, and by Father Patrick O'Connor of Dookinella church. The discussion began a bit hesitantly. Local people sat in the primary school pupils' chairs.

'Are you going to consecrate the graves, Father?' I asked.

'Bless them,' he said. 'We're going to bless them.'

I began to breathe more easily.

'They're angels, really,' Father O'Connor added. My shoulders relaxed. Born in Roscrea, County Tipperary, he had been away in England for more than forty years before retiring to Achill and, he said, he had been unaware of the *cillíní*. He added, 'They're holy places. The danger is that maybe the sites would be lost.'

Over the next several weeks, many Dookinella residents worked on *Páistí Marbha*, clearing the land of rocks and boulders, raking it, carrying buckets of soil, covering the *cillín* with the soil and marking the border of the graves with white stones gathered and brought to the site in a tractor. The image of people carrying stones and buckets of soil towards the eroding graves of unbaptised infants on the edge of the sea was a scene from another century. Brent videotaped the work being done and wrote music to accompany the footage. A local man built a small monument and a statue of an angel was placed on top. Someone made a cross of stones, placing them on the ground, out of the wind. Father O'Connor and Father Gilligan blessed the graves in a special ceremony attended by about two hundred people. The following words were inscribed on a plaque:

Páistí Marbha
In remembrance of
the babies buried here
Angels in heaven
Blessed on 21-5-2000

Now when the moon climbs over Minaun and rises up over the infants' graves, its light shines down on the small monument and the cross of stones. During the day I see visitors, hill-walkers and island residents stop at the *cillín*, perched on the edge of Keel Bay. They read the plaque and pay their respects, admiring the views of Croghaun and the wider North Atlantic. They no longer stomp on the babies' graves unknowingly on their way up Minaun. They stand on a site which has been blessed, and they reflect on the lives unlived and the treatment the infants received after death.

People were sorry when the work on the *cillín* ended. It had created a rare unity of purpose, a sense of community and the satisfaction that comes from literally being on the side of the angels.

'Guess what?' Conor said. 'The cows are back.'

'How many this time?' I asked.

'Five.'

There are two large fields and a section of commonage between our house and the *cillín*, and in the first Jack McDonnell keeps his biscuit-coloured cows when the grass is long enough. The cows make great neighbours; they munch grass and mind their own business during the day and come to the top of the field at night to look in the windows and say hello to the humans. Sometimes they rub their backs against the electricity pole; at other times they rest. We are always happy to see them.

Where there's muck, there's luck.

I was ringing Conor on my mobile from the Harding Hotel in Dublin, my home away from home when I work in the *Irish Times* newsroom in Dublin. After a few years I ended my job-share and began to work three days a week at the paper, while Conor and Brent stayed in Achill full-time. I travelled to Dublin on Wednesday, heading straight into work, and returned to Achill on Saturday morning.

The Harding is a quirky budget hotel on Fishamble Street,

across from Christ Church Cathedral, about a fifteen-minute walk from the *Irish Times* office on D'Olier Street. It is handy for work and for getting the train from Heuston station back to Castlebar early on a Saturday morning. I have come to know the staff, although they mostly see the back of my head as I'm passing through. The manager, Áine Hickey, was born in County Laois and raised in Leixlip, County Kildare. Her grandmother, Elizabeth Hickey, who appears to have been somewhat eccentric, wrote *The Green Cockatrice*, a book about Shakespeare, under the pseudonym Basil Iske (pronounced Ike). Elizabeth Hickey lived in Skryne Castle, in Skryne, County Meath, where she wrote a number of historical books, including *Skryne and the Early Normans*, *The Legend of Tara*, and *Clonard – The Story of an Early Irish Monastery*.

Emma Murphy books my accommodation for six months at a time. In autumn and winter I stay in a quiet room on a higher floor facing the courtyard; in spring and summer she puts me in a room overlooking Christ Church Cathedral. I need to leave for work at about 3 p.m. and rarely return before eleven. The Harding experience is oddly reminiscent of my years in 5 East 51st Street, Apartment 5C, near St Patrick's in New York: I'm a great woman for staying beside the cathedrals.

My unusual lifestyle prompts questions from colleagues.

'Where do you eat breakfast?'

'A place called Chill.'

'Where do you eat lunch?'

'La Mère Zou.'

Copper Alley, which runs through the Harding, dates back to the thirteenth century and follows the route of an earlier Viking street. In the fifteenth century it was known as Preston's Lane. A plaque inside the hotel states that by the early seventeenth century it became known as Copper Alley, from the money minted there. The alley was famous for its taverns and eating houses; it was home to a brothel run by a woman known as Darkey Kelly, who was tried for a capital offence and burned at the stake in St Stephen's Green in 1746. A pub is named after her now. Handel's *Messiah* was performed for the first time in 1742 in the nearby Music Hall; a passage was opened from the alley to the music hall on Fishamble Street.

Diagonally opposite the Harding are the gleaming Civic Offices on Wood Quay, where I marched with thousands of Friends of Medieval Dublin in 1979 in an attempt to save the Viking site from destruction. In Ireland on the Watson Fellowship at the time, I read about the controversy in *Hibernia*. The protesters sang 'Molly Malone' through the streets during the demonstration against Dublin Corporation's development plans. Another song sung; another battle lost.

Around 3 p.m., when it's time to leave the hotel, I step on to the pavement and begin my walk to work, pondering the question: is it more dangerous to be a pedestrian in Dublin or a passenger in a motor-car in Mayo? Would I be more likely to be hit by a four-wheel-drive vehicle jumping on the cracked footpaths of the city-centre or by a Mayo motorist on a provisional licence driving towards me over the unbroken white line? It's a bit like the question a child asks: 'Mum, which way do you want to die, by fire or by ice?' The answer is: 'Neither.' Twin hazards confront me on a weekly basis in my bicoastal life. Repeatedly I ask: why has being a pedestrian in Dublin become a form of urban combat? And why can't Mayo drivers stay on their own side of the road?

I walk up Fishamble Street, cross at the pedestrian lights and turn left on Lord Edward Street as oil trucks and buses rumble by. Beyond Dublin Castle an ambulance screams past; I say a short prayer for all cyclists and pedestrians. Mind the buses and the lorries. Mind the broken footpaths. I wonder why so many people spit on the street. Heading towards Trinity College, I see one of my favourite Dublin street signs: *Mórshraíd Sheoirse Theas* (George's Street Great South).

There is time so I call into Books Upstairs on College Green, where a man in an enormous fur hat rushes in and pulls a great hardback volume of T. S. Eliot from the shelves. Maurice Earls spots me. 'Still reading,' he says kindly. Yes, still calling into the bookshop after all these years, and still reading, although now, as I approach my fiftieth birthday, I have three pairs of eyeglasses: one for reading a book, newspaper or page proof; one for looking at the computer; and one for crossing the road.

'Anyway, enjoy your flamenco,' an Irish lad says to a Spanish girl in front of Trinity, near the sign with the words 'Cyclists dismount'. The city-centre is teeming now: how times have changed. I stood lonely as a cloud in that same spot in 1979 for the St Patrick's Day parade, watching twelve Americans in Burberry coats walk sadly down the street in the rain.

There are two more sets of pedestrian lights. Mind the cars. Mind the buses. I cross College Street and pass the Westin Hotel. Not there yet. The trickiest corner awaits, the right turn off Westmoreland Street on to Fleet Street, where taxis and buses have taken aim at *Irish Times* journalists for years. If you don't take an artful look left as you cross, you're a goner. Go past the bus fumes, eroded kerbs and smokers forced out on to the sidewalk. The sign appears:

THE IRISH TIMES
EDITORIAL
AND
WORKS ENTRANCE

Go in through the familiar twelve-foot doors, up five steps, pass security and take the lift to the second floor. I've made it to work, and I'm still alive.

Seven or eight hours later I take a taxi back to the Harding, avoiding the baying revellers of Temple Bar. I look at the moon, and yearn to be with the man and the boy who live under it.

'David Beckham owns a piece of the moon,' Conor said in

the back of the car once, coming home on the winding road from Mulranny in the dark.

'Who sold it to him?' his friend, John Lavelle, asked.

On the brief journey to Fishamble Street, the taxi-driver says, 'You haven't lost your accent.'

'And you haven't lost yours,' I wearily reply.

By Friday night I'm looking forward to the next morning, when I'll be back in the arms of Iarnród Éireann, heading home on the early train. I'll be able to stay in Achill until the following Wednesday morning.

Irish Rail has spent one billion euro on line improvements: the Dublin to Castlebar travel time has been cut to three hours and fifteen minutes, the old smokers' car is gone, and we have been promised new rolling stock and five trips daily. If only the engines wouldn't break down.

9

In Search of Heinrich Böll

'Guten Tag,' I said in my best Boston-accented German. 'Is René Böll there?'

I heard a giggle at the other end of the phone in Cologne.

'One moment, please,' a young woman said in German-accented English.

René Böll came to the phone and greeted me warmly. A painter and photographer, he is the son of Heinrich Böll, the Nobel Prize-winning German writer who owned a cottage in Achill for many years. We had been in touch when I was writing various articles over the years about the Böll Cottage, in the village of Dugort, which has been in use as a writers' and artists' residency since 1992.

It was about ten days before Christmas 2004. A death notice had appeared in *The Times* of London for his mother Annemarie, who died on 15 November aged ninety-four. Annemarie Böll had been a translator of many works of literature in her own right, and she had made the Böll Cottage residency possible. Achill, and the larger world of literature in translation, owes her a great deal.

I read the clipping from *The Times* of London and rang *The Irish Times* in Dublin. I told Paddy Smyth, then obits editor, that Heinrich Böll's widow had died, and that she had been a translator of many Irish writers. 'We should run an obituary,' I ventured.

'You do it,' he said.

'She died a month ago.'

'That's okay. I'll need it by Thursday afternoon,' Paddy said. I looked at the calendar: it was Tuesday morning. He asked me to remember the essentials: her date of birth, date of death, names of her parents and names of her children. 'Cheers,' he said and hung up.

I wasn't in the D'Olier Street office with its powerful computer system, which could access information on the internet in seconds. I'd have to put together the obituary at home in Dookinella, with a phone line that crackled in the rain and a computer with much slower access to the Web. There were other practical problems: if we experienced a mid-winter power cut, as we occasionally did at that time of year, the computer would power down and eat any unsaved copy, and I'd be unable to transmit the piece to Dublin on deadline.

The only thing to do was to proceed as though there would be no power cuts, and to phone René and ask for his help with background information about his mother; he agreed instantly and gave me his e-mail address. I sent a series of questions to him from Achill and waited for his replies, as the clock ticked and the deadline approached.

The first question was: 'What were the names of Annemarie's father and mother?'

René e-mailed the following reply: 'Her father was (Ober-kommissär der k.k. Oesterreichischen Staatbahnen) Eduard Cech (25.2.1867-10.3.1916) her mother Stephanie Cech, born Hagen (26.12.1883-25.12.1915).'

I looked at the response in dismay. I picked up the phone and dialled his number in Germany.

'René, what does Oberkommissär der k.k. Osterreichischen Staatbahnen mean?' I asked, stumbling over the pronunciation of the long German words.

'He was employed by the railway.'

'Okay, thanks. *The Times* of London said she translated more than two hundred works of literature, which sounds like an awful lot. Is that right?'

'More like one hundred, make it more than one hundred.'

I adjusted the figure on my computer screen.

'Do you have a photograph of your mother?'

'Yes. I can e-mail it to you.'

'Good. Can you also e-mail it directly to the paper? If there's a gale, I may lose power and not be able to transmit it from here.'

'Yes, I can do that.'

I gave René the e-mail address of the photographers in *The Irish Times*. 'Thanks. I'll phone you back if I need anything else.'

I hung up.

The wind was picking up under the Minaun Cliffs. I began to save my copy every couple of paragraphs. If we lost electricity, I would be unable to finish my research on the Web.

I studied the dates of birth and death René had given me for Annemarie's parents and realised that her mother had died on Christmas Day 1915 when Annemarie was five years old. Her father died less than three months later, on 10 March 1916. The story of a woman's life was unfolding.

My next questions were: 'Where was she born? Educated?'

His e-mailed answer was: 'My mother was born on 23 June 1910 in Pilsen, today Czechia (sorry I don't know if this is the correct English word), in this times Austria. She grown up bilingual Czech-German and came in 1916, when her father died, to Cologne, where she was educated in the gymnasium and studied teacher.'

Good. We were getting somewhere. The lights in my house flickered, the wind howled and rain began to lash the windows of my attic office.

'I know she married your father in 1942. When did she help him on the reworked German translation of *The Catcher in the Rye*?' I e-mailed back.

'They made the translation in the early Sixties, it was

published in 1963. She was the translator, my father helped her. She translated also many Irish books, among others: Behan, Eilís Dillon,' he replied.

We were rolling now. There was valour in René's efforts to translate his mother's life into English. I had a final question. 'What was her opinion of Achill – did she enjoy it as much as your father?'

His response: 'We all loved or still love Achill, we all enjoyed it so much, it was our home for many years and I still love to come to Achill. I will be there in June next year, making studies for my paintings. I will try to phone you later on. Thank you. René.'

I made a few more calls to Cologne and re-read the London *Times* obituary and my previous pieces on the Bölls in Achill. I could hardly hear the sound of my own voice for the wind and the rain. I worked on the piece day and night. On Thursday afternoon I finished the obituary, pressed 'send' on my home computer and sighed with relief. Minutes later my house was plunged into darkness: the dreaded power cut. The gale blasted the roof and the south-west corner of my house. The roof tiles rattled and the rain pelted the windows, but my piece had made it to Dublin.

René e-mailed a photograph of his mother from Cologne to *The Irish Times*, and the obituary and colour photo, taken by René, appeared in the paper on 18 December 2004.

The effort was a tribute to a woman who had survived Hitler, poverty, the deaths of her infant son and later her husband, to make a significant contribution of her own to literature in translation. She specialised in Irish writers, making the works of Behan, Synge, Shaw and Flann O'Brien available to a large and enthusiastic German public. She also translated the work of the American writers O. Henry and Bernard Malamud.

As René was doing his best to tell me, Annemarie Böll was born in June 1910 in Pilsen, in what is now the Czech Republic, the middle child of a railway worker, Eduard Cech, and his German wife, Stephanie. The family was bilingual. Annemarie's mother died when she was five and her father died three months later. She and one of her two brothers went to live with their German grandparents in Cologne, where she trained as a teacher.

She married Heinrich Böll, a soldier and native of Cologne, in 1942, at the height of the Second World War. It was a time of hardship for the couple. Their first son, Christoph, died in infancy in October 1945 as the result of a lack of proper medication. Raimund, René and Vincent were born in 1947, 1948 and 1950, respectively, and grew up 'in the rubble of Cologne', as Heinrich Böll later wrote. Raimund, an artist and sculptor, died in 1981.

Heinrich Böll was born into a Catholic pacifist family in Cologne in 1917. His life was wracked by war – he hated Hitler, but he was conscripted and served on the Russian and French fronts. He was wounded four times before he was captured by American soldiers and sent to a prisoner-of-war camp. After the war he became an independent force in a demoralised Germany; he was a defender of intellectual freedom and president of the international PEN writers' group. His many novels include *The Train Was on Time* (1949); *Billiards at Half-past Nine* (1959); *The Clown* (1963); and *The Lost Honour of Katharina Blum* (1974). In 1981 he published a memoir, *What's to Become of the Boy? or, Something to Do with Books*. After his experience of war, he would remain on guard against totalitarianism of all sorts for the rest of his life.

The Train Was on Time opens with a quotation from Antoine de Saint-Exupéry's *Pilote de Guerre:*

> I have known many adventures in my time: the creation of postal routes, Sahara rebellions, South America … but war is not really an adventure at all, it is only a substitute for adventure … War is a disease. Like typhus.

Recognition for Böll was slow in coming when he started writing full-time. 'So much of Heinrich's work was written on my kitchen table,' Annemarie once remarked. She assisted and supported her husband professionally and he acknowledged her contribution. While reworking a German translation of J. D. Salinger's *The Catcher in the Rye* in the early 1960s, he told his publisher that it was 'an excellent exercise in style for me but very hard labour – although ninety per cent of the work is being done by my wife'.

In 1972 Böll was awarded the Nobel Prize in Literature. In an autobiographical note for the Nobel Foundation he stated: 'In 1942 I married Annemarie Cech, who has been irreplaceable, not only as my wife and companion, and not only as fellow experiencer and fellow sufferer in the fascist drama during the Nazi reign in Germany, but also for her critical awareness of language.'

Heinrich Böll came to Achill Island for the first time in 1955 with Annemarie and their three young sons. He had visited Ireland a year earlier but had not travelled to Mayo. His *Irisches Tagebuch (Irish Journal),* published in 1957 and translated into English ten years later, propelled generations of German visitors to Ireland, especially to Achill. It is a portrait of Ireland and of Mayo in a much simpler time. Two framed, translated letters, which hang in the small study in the Böll Cottage today, capture his first impressions of the island. He wrote the first letter on 4 June 1955 when, after a three-day journey, his family arrived in Achill.

The letter is addressed to his father and sister, Mechtild Böll (1907–72), known as Tilde. The Eichs he mentions were a German couple, both writers:

Keel, June 4, 1955

Dear father, dear Tilde:
 We had a very pleasant journey, and arrived yesterday evening precisely at 8.00 p.m. after a trip of

three days. There was one thing which went wrong: my typewriter does not work (a porter dropped it). Both ferry-trips were wonderful, the children were excited and made it without any difficulties. A bit wearing was only the last part, the bus-trip from Westport to here: almost three hours. The landscape is wonderful, the house is quite beautiful, roomy and comfortable, we have eight beautiful beds to sleep in – and our chimney fire burns wonderfully: the children and Christel are sitting in front of it, and Annemarie takes a nap. In a minute I will try to repair the typewriter because I have to work. The next mechanic lives about three bus-hours away.

We are all very happy here: the children have a great appetite and enjoy everything very much, especially the donkeys, the ocean, and the chimney fire: René has already fully recovered. The children are playing happily. It is peaceful and beautiful, and everything is much cheaper. Annemarie did her first shopping. It has been raining all day, but we don't mind at all, because our living room is cozy and warm. My only concern is the typewriter.

A huge amount of turf has just been delivered: now nothing can happen to us anymore, and the hosts were positively excited that we are Catholic.

Best greetings to all (Alfred, Alois, and Coin), especially the Eichs. (We also have received all of our luggage.)

Many happy greetings from all of us.

Hein and Raimund

Two days later, on 6 June 1955, he wrote another letter to his father and sister about his typewriter and his experience of travelling across Ireland by train without having any Irish money to pay his train fare. Readers of *Irish Journal* will be familiar with the episode, the basis for one of the finest sections of the book. The Fleischmann to whom he refers is his friend in Dublin, George Fleischmann (1912–95), an Austrian cameraman and film-maker who had been a photographer in the Luftwaffe. Fleischmann was interned in Ireland during the war after a forced landing, and stayed.

Keel, Achill Island
June 6, 1955

Dear father, dear Tilde, we have spent the whole day in an adventurous way repairing the typewriter, and – as you see – fixed it perfectly. This misfortune has thus been removed, for the time being. Yesterday (Sunday) we had wonderful weather, also today it is very nice, only a bit windy, and we spent a long time at the beach: for the time being we are the only strangers in this village (which is by the way bigger than we thought, about 200 inhabitants): there are enough shops and every week a big truck with groceries comes. And everything is really cheap: a huge loaf of bread costs 65 pfennig, butter 2,20 DM. A half pound of tea 1,80 DM etc. Only our house was not yet fully usable: the electrical stove was not yet installed (we have electrical light), and thus we had our first larger meals at the Gallaghers, who are very very nice (eight children and one hotel!). The people here in the village are all very nice. We could test this because we had problems with our money: in Dublin, while transferring from the boat to the train, we did not have enough time to change money. In addition the banks opened only at 10 a.m., and our train left already at 8.30 a.m. After a long exchange which Annemarie had with the chief of the train station we were allowed to ride from Dublin to Westport with an unpaid ticket: Six hours, and we were optimistic enough to believe to get money exchanged in Westport.

There we were able to get away from the chief of the train station after long exchanges, who had been informed in the meantime about our existence over the phone; then we chased the bank employees (it was three o'clock in the afternoon) out of their siesta, only to learn that they could not exchange my money, but that they had to transfer it to Dublin. And if I were lucky, they maintained I would receive it exchanged on Wednesday (that is two days later). I had no choice but to leave my entire money in Westport and to drive with the last shillings to Keel. In Keel we had the same problem again. Then I called Fleischmann in Dublin (with loaned money) and asked him to post money. The order arrived at noon around two o'clock, but the post-office had no money. It was for this reason that we received the 10 pounds which Fleischmann had sent me, as late as today; O lovely Ireland, I still have not yet paid my rail tickets.

Do not worry if the mail is a little bit slow: nothing works here very fast: even the prayer in church yesterday was slow and pure.

Best greetings to all, also to the Eichs.

Hein, Annemarie and the children

In 1958 the Bölls bought the cottage in the secluded village of Dugort, finding solace in Achill's remoteness and wild beauty. The island seems to have had a healing power for them. René recalls his father reading in the white, horseshoe-shaped house surrounded by fuchsia and flax. He and his brothers, Vincent and Raimund, spent long hours outside in the sea, exploring mountains and bogs, or using their boat on Blacksod Bay. This last activity worried their parents, René said.

Heinrich Böll is remembered on Achill as a very gentle, somewhat shy person, a totally understated man. He wore a beret, he smoked continuously, and he and his family walked and walked, no matter what, in their German all-weather gear. The family lived in the cottage periodically for twenty-seven years, until Böll's death in June 1985. Four years later, Annemarie made her last visit to the island, aged seventy-nine. She took the boat from Achill to Clare Island with René and his family.

Achill Island has seen unrelenting development since Böll's era, and in these prosperous days roads and new homes casually desecrate mountains. The island is undergoing a process of suburbanisation: large houses and holiday home developments blight the elemental landscape. Some villages are ruined; others are under threat. Not all of Böll's Achill is gone, however. It takes more than bulldozers and concrete-mixers to destroy thousands of years of human history. The big sky, the sandy beaches, the cliffs and the light on the sea continue to uplift, as does the contentment of people minding their own patches. A walk to the beach at Anach on Blacksod Bay, unchanged since the Ice Age, is an otherworldly experience. Salmon fishermen used to go there in summertime, living in a hut in Keel. And Böll's description in *Irish Journal* of the atmosphere in the deserted village on the southern slope of Slievemore still rings true today:

> Here no one razed anything to the ground, and the softer parts of abandoned dwellings are left to feed the wind, the rain, the sun, and time, and after sixty, seventy, or a hundred years all that is left is half-finished buildings from which no carpenter will ever again hang his wreath to celebrate the completion of a house: this, then, is what a human habitation looks

like when it has been left in peace after death.

In 1991 Annemarie and René Böll offered the use of their cottage as a writers' and artists' retreat, and since then more than one hundred and fifty people from all over the world have benefited from their generosity. They have come from Ireland and Northern Ireland, England, Scotland, Wales, France, Germany, Austria, Hungary and the United States. Others have travelled from Croatia, Russia, Poland, Canada, Belgium, Bulgaria, China, Denmark, Israel, Ecuador, Holland and Switzerland, seeking the inspiration Böll found in Achill.

Some are former soldiers themselves, veterans of the Vietnam War. Many have come through association with Kevin Bowen, a Vietnam veteran who is director of the William Joiner Center for the Study of War and Social Consequences at the University of Massachusetts in Boston. He stayed at the cottage in 1997 and 1999 and was so taken with the island that he built his own Achill house in Caban. Kevin encouraged Vietnamese poet Nguyen Quang Thieu to come to Achill. Thieu, from a village in North Vietnam, lived through the war and grew up under the bombing; after the war he was chosen to study literature in Cuba for three years. On Achill, in the Cyril Gray Memorial Hall, Thieu read in Vietnamese from his work *The Women Carry River Water* while Kevin stood beside him, translating the poems into English.

Little did I know when I bought the house in Achill that there would be a steady stream of poets arriving from Massachusetts to stay in the cottage, among them Fred Marchant, professor of English and director of the creative writing programme at Suffolk University in Boston, author of *Tipping Point*, and one of the first US Marine officers to be discharged honourably in 1970 as a conscientious objector to the Vietnam War. He was stationed on Okinawa at the time and had not yet gone to Vietnam.

'I felt as if I was under the roof of a wise friend, one who understood the moral complexities of being born into a terrible regime and time,' Fred said of his stay in the Böll Cottage.

A long list of well-known Irish writers has stayed in the cottage. Anne Enright worked there on her novel *What Are You Like?* Hugo Hamilton, author of *The Speckled People*, a memoir about his German mother and his Irish-language-obsessed father, stayed in the house, as have poets Gabriel Rosenstock and Cathal Ó Searcaigh.

Most of the visiting writers and artists work in the study overlooking Blacksod Bay and walk on the beaches and bogs. Many residents give readings or talks, or visit schools during their stay. In summer the cottage is a place of pilgrimage for German tourists, who travel a great distance to a remote place in search of Heinrich Böll.

In 2001, Annemarie Böll offered to sell the cottage to the local Böll committee for £100,000, thereby ensuring its legacy as an artists' residence and a memorial to her husband. A tenacious and ambitious community effort to procure the funds was initiated by the Böll committee chairman, Dr Edward King, whose late mother, Clodagh King, had been a friend of Heinrich Böll and a founding member of the Böll committee.

Tom McNamara, a Böll committee member and owner of the Boley House restaurant in Keel, spoke to me on several occasions about the pressing need to purchase the cottage. It was becoming apparent that Ireland, and in particular Achill, would lose a literary landmark and a cultural attraction of international importance if the committee did not buy the house. At work in *The Irish Times* I ran into Helen Meany, who was overseeing the arts page, and told her what was happening.

'Would you like a piece about the Böll Cottage for the arts page?' I asked.

Helen uttered the magic words: 'I'd love one.'

David Sleator was despatched two hundred miles to take a photograph. *The Irish Times* was giving the project its imprimatur. I got to work.

'I'd better write a letter to the Minister,' Denis Gallagher, former Minister for the Gaeltacht and a native of the Currane peninsula, had said when he heard that an article was going to appear in *The Irish Times*. The letter was written, the article appeared, further contacts were made and a meeting was set up with the Minister for the Arts, Heritage, Gaeltacht and the Islands, Síle de Valera, at the opening of Turlough Park House, outside Castlebar, County Mayo, on 9 September 2001, two days before the hijacked planes went into the World Trade Center. It was an extremely hot day in that period known in Achill as 'the Keel man's fortnight', when the traditional spell of good, Indian summer weather in September allowed the Keel people to take in their hay. Denis Gallagher led the Böll Cottage delegation. A courtly man of the old school and a fluent Irish-speaker, he had known Síle de Valera since she was a baby. He missed his first All-Ireland hurling final in forty years to attend the meeting.

Among the large delegation were the committee's long-time secretary, John McHugh; Tom McNamara; poet and publisher John F. Deane, a founding member of the Böll committee, who had suggested in the early 1990s that the cottage be used as an artists' residency; Peter Hynes, director of services for Mayo County Council, which had long supported the project; and Paul Durcan, who wrote most of his poetry collection *Greetings to Our Friends in Brazil* during a month-long stay in what he called 'an ex-soldier's house on the side of the big mountain'.

Each person spoke in turn to the minister, presenting the case for purchasing the cottage and preserving it as an artists' residence.

A few weeks later, word came from Denis Gallagher that Síle de Valera had approved £60,000 for the purchase of the cottage. In a pre-Celtic Tiger Ireland this gesture would have been almost unimaginable. The local committee was over its biggest hurdle. With £30,000 from Mayo County Council and £10,000 from its own funds, it was able to purchase the cottage.

It had seemed 'an impossible dream', Edward King said. 'Without Denis's input, it simply wouldn't have happened,' Tom McNamara said.

Within a short time Denis Gallagher had died. To the parish of Achill and Currane it was the death of a chieftain. Hundreds of people attended the wake in Glór na dTonn (Sound of the Waves), the community centre in Currane for which Denis had been instrumental in obtaining the funding. It was the largest funeral I had seen in Ireland, spilling over from the church into the community centre next door. The Taoiseach, Bertie Ahern, attended, calling Denis 'a giant of the west'. Father Gilligan, who had been friendly with Denis for forty years, celebrated the funeral Mass, during which he looked at the Taoiseach and mentioned the need for broadband for Achill, an issue Denis had been working on when he died.

The Böll Cottage closed for badly-needed renovation after funding was obtained for its refurbishment.

Mrs Violet McDowell, of Gray's Hotel in Dugort, Achill, was asked to host an afternoon meal for up to one hundred people on 23 February 2005 following the official reopening of the cottage. No bother to Vi, just days before her ninety-fifth birthday. She proceeded to organise the reception, for which she would need a staff of nine, and she ordered a special commemorative cake from Dublin.

The Böll committee, reconstituted as a registered company called the Achill Heinrich Böll Association, asked for light refreshments, but aides to Minister for the Arts John O'Donoghue, who was going to perform the opening, said that the minister required a proper meal. In a flash it went from finger food to feast, with the hostess characteristically unperturbed. Vi turned out a meal of biblical proportions.

'I don't want people to find out my age,' Vi said, to laughter and applause from the gathering of more than one hundred at the reception, including John O'Donoghue; the German ambassador to Ireland, Dr Gottfried Haas, and his wife Béatrice, who had braved Siberian conditions that morning to drive from Dublin to Achill in snow and sleet; representatives of Mayo County Council; and island residents and visitors, among them painters, writers and composers, some of whom had stayed in the cottage. Vi stood for a long time, smiling and observing her guests, before making her way round the dining room for a chat.

Vi was born in 1910 in a house at the foot of Slievemore mountain, the daughter of William Robert Gray and Rebecca McNally. Her father was an engineer with Lawrence of Arabia, Based in Cairo, he made a survey of Egypt from airplane photographs of battle areas. Her mother was a native of Achill.

In 1940 she married Arthur McDowell, of the Ulster Bank, from Banbridge, County Down. The couple spent much of their married life in Tuam, County Galway. Vi's mother ran a guest house in Achill called The Seaview and, following Arthur's retirement from the bank in 1970, Vi and Arthur took over the business, renaming it Gray's. They developed it over twenty-five years, earning a listing in the *Egon Ronay Guide*.

After Arthur died in 1995, Vi continued to run Gray's, where she remains to this day, a tireless storyteller and hostess, the midnight lady of Dugort, extending hospitality to her guests.

It was a trilingual day in Dugort. At the official opening ceremony in the cottage's courtyard there were speeches in Irish, German and English, punctuated by birdsong, applause and the occasional honking of a car security system. The Mayo flag flew and the pipe band played. The speeches were long but worthy; the sense of occasion was stronger than the need to be brief or entertaining. We stood in cold but brilliantly sunny conditions beneath a Paul Henry sky, enjoying a reprieve from howling winds and horizontal rain.

Minister O'Donoghue looked up briefly towards the sun and tried to imagine how a survivor of the Second World War must have felt coming to Achill, 'this exceptionally beautiful part of

County Mayo'. Standing in the courtyard of the writer's former residence, he was able to appreciate the inspiration and peace Böll had found.

It was a proud day for all involved in the Böll Cottage project for almost fifteen years, and an opportunity to salute Heinrich and Annemarie Böll, whose altruism enabled so many writers and artists to enjoy their former island home.

10

What Melville Knew

News that John Moriarty had triple cancer – in the liver, bowel and prostate – came as a shock to his friends throughout Ireland in January 2006, but to hear him talking about it to Joe Duffy on *Liveline* in April was somehow reassuring. Even more encouraging was the fact that, with strong new drugs and treatments, his doctors were prepared, as John put it, 'to put up a fight'. His friends in Dublin, Kerry and along the west coast already had circled the wagons, sending text messages to one another with the latest bulletins about his condition. Eileen Moore gave up her job to care for him. The man himself took all our phone calls, patiently giving updates, describing the hospital scenes, and signing off with his characteristic 'God bless'. Hearing the diagnosis had been traumatic, but it appeared that his doctors did not consider it a death sentence. He had a chance for a longer life, one which could be of good quality. Why else submit to the chemotherapy drip?

When I spoke to John on the phone on a sunny day in May 2006, he was proofreading his massive book on Europe, *Night Journey to Buddh Gaia*. His voice was strong and, despite a pain in his arm and the profound fatigue that results from chemotherapy, he was, in his own words, 'optimistic on either side of death'.

John Moriarty is a philosopher, writer and mystic from north Kerry. His mother's early assessment of him may have contained a certain bleakness: 'What with his drainpipe trousers and long hair, he doesn't even look like a fact of life,' but her son John went on to write *Nostos,* from the Greek word for homecoming, a 698-page autobiography published in 2001 which Aidan Carl Mathews called 'the greatest Irish book since *Ulysses*'. Few who attended University College Dublin with John, who took a first-class honours degree in philosophy, would disagree with the view that he has one of the best minds in Ireland.

He is the man who reawakened my interest in American literature after nearly twenty years in Ireland, who brought me back to my days as an English major at Williams College in the 1970s, sitting in a classroom staring at Mount Greylock with its whale-shaped peak or poring over the pages of *Moby-Dick*. He explained Herman Melville's diagnosis of the western psyche to me, trying to help me understand why America and western Europe are in the state they are in today. He described what had been going on in my own backyard in the Berkshires of Massachusetts and he attempted to teach me what Melville knew, to help me reclaim my American inheritance in both its positive and negative aspects after so many years away. He was instructive about the profound changes taking place, both positive and negative, in my adoptive and ancestral homeland of Ireland.

I interviewed John for the first time on Clare Island, which meant driving from Achill to Roonagh pier and getting the boat. I had begun to read *Nostos* and had been amazed by its depth and erudition, its grace and independence of thought; it struck me that, while he might not claim the title, John seemed to be an heir to Herman Melville.

'I'm nervous,' I confided to a friend, before heading to Clare Island. 'He's smart.'

The drive along the Mayo coast was a labour of love, and the sea sparkled as I left Achill and headed towards Mulranny and Newport. Westport gleamed, tidy and proud. In Murrisk I saluted Croagh Patrick and slowed down to admire John Behan's bronze sculpture of a coffin ship in the Famine Memorial Park, a lonely work set incongruously close to the busy road. The day was brilliantly sunny and fresh, ideal for my trip. Beyond Louisburgh I turned right for the pier at Roonagh. I took my seat on O'Malley's *Island Princess* and watched Mayo county councillors in jackets and ties board O'Grady's *Pirate Queen*. Crewmen's voices rose above the engine as the ferry rumbled into Clew Bay.

John stood waiting on the pier on Clare Island, tall and contemplative, with his distinctive mop of curly white hair. He was visiting the island to take part in the Bard summer school on Irish myths, founded ten years ago by Ellen O'Malley-Dunlop, a Dublin psychotherapist and descendant of Granuaile, the sixteenth-century Pirate Queen of Connaught believed to be buried in St Brigid's Abbey on the island. The abbey contains rare medieval wall-paintings, which were restored in a painstaking project that took more than ten years. The only known Irish image of a medieval organ was uncovered during the conservation work.

'Up Kerry,' he called to a passer-by outside the community centre. We walked past the hotel and sat on a cliff overlooking the bay with spectacular views of Achill, Mulranny and Croagh Patrick. He identified the flowers around us: 'purple wild mountain thyme, eye-bright, regarded traditionally as being a cure for blindness, dwarf ferns, trefoil, beautiful grasses and unopened dandelions'. We were sitting in 'literally a herbal meadow', he observed.

'Are you writing anything, John?'

'There are three things on the go at the moment, one big book and two smaller works.'

One of the shorter books, *Ailiu Iath n-hErend, Invoking Ireland*, which picks up where Yeats and Lady Gregory left off, was published in the autumn of 2005 and introduced at the Clifden Arts Festival. In the book John retells twenty of Ireland's oldest tales from the eighth and ninth centuries, having read them in the original Irish. The book's title comes from 'I Invoke the

Land of Ireland', among the first words spoken in Irish in Ireland by Amhairghin Glungheal, the poet at the head of the fleet as the Celts came up Kenmare Bay.

'What he's doing is he's calling the rivers, he's calling the mountains, he's calling the animals, he's calling the grass, he's calling the trees, he's calling everything over on to his side,' John said.

> Now that's what I'm trying to do in this book. I'm trying to reinvoke the land of Ireland, and my way of reinvoking the land of Ireland is to bring back some of the ancient stories and to see if there isn't both a conscience and a consciousness there that is really the ancient soul of Ireland and that we would do well to recover. My sense is that it is not a question of inventing Ireland, it's a question of discovering an Ireland that's there. Douglas Hyde did not invent Ireland; he uncovered an Ireland in *The Love Songs of Connaught*. Synge didn't invent the Aran Islands; he went there and discovered them. Also Yeats and Lady Gregory.

John was born in 1938 and educated at St Michael's, Listowel, where he studied Greek and Latin. After teaching English literature for six years at the University of Manitoba in Canada, which he found 'an ideal human society, an environment in which you could absolutely prosper', he returned to Ireland in 1971. He has lived in beautiful, remote places, sometimes in quite primitive circumstances. He spent twenty-three years in Connemara and he has lived in Coolies, Muckross, County Kerry, for the past ten. He does not own a car, a television, a computer or a typewriter. For years he travelled by bus or train around the country to give talks. He writes most days, in longhand, even now that he is ill.

In addition to *Nostos* and *Invoking Ireland*, John is the author of *Dreamtime* (1994), and the trilogy *Turtle Was Gone a Long Time: Crossing the Kedron* (1996), *Horsehead Nebula Neighing* (1997) and *Anaconda Canoe* (1998). He has read and seemingly ingested all the great books and he quotes freely and frequently from them. His encyclopaedic mind roams from ancient Greece to the crisis facing the modern world, namely the survival of our planet.

'I am heartbroken about what is happening to the planet,' he told me on Clare Island. He continued:

> We have done so much ecological havoc to the world. We are now AIDS virus to the Earth. We are doing to the Earth what the AIDS virus does to the human body: we are breaking down its immune system. And I don't know that the Earth can survive our presence in it. In the meantime, Ireland has become another Japan. Dublin is another Tokyo, with the amount of concrete that's being poured all over the place. I personally do not want to move about the world in a bullet train. We're going to have a bullet train from Dingle to Puck Fair.

He said, 'I believe that we need a Naissance, not a Renaissance. Collectively we need to be radically original in our thinking. The Greeks can't help us this time.'

I asked him how invoking Ireland could work in the present day, when one in ten people in the country was a foreign national.

He replied:

> There is now a new coming ashore into Ireland, in the way that the Vikings came, the Celts came, the Megalith builders came. I would hope for the people who are now coming to Ireland, I want to say to them that I hope that we have a great story for

you to come ashore into, not just another economy or into Ireland.com, and that maybe in time you can find that you can inhabit our great story because we have begun to inhabit it architecturally, poetically, in literature, in all kinds of ways.

Half-way through our interview John moved from the idea of the ideal human society – which he found at the University of Manitoba and which I found at Williams College – to the deck of a whaling ship, where Herman Melville received his education. Out of the blue he mentioned *Moby-Dick,* calling it 'one of the great books of the world'.

I looked up from my notebook. It had been twenty-seven years since I had been an undergraduate and heard anyone discussing *Moby-Dick* seriously. Too long to go without Melville.

John said: '*Moby-Dick* is the greatest diagnosis of the western psyche that we have, infinitely better than Hegel's diagnosis, infinitely better than Marx.'

Our time was running short and I had a boat to catch, but I was determined to interview him again and ask him about *Moby-Dick*. At that point I had been in the news business for almost twenty-five years, seventeen of them at *The Irish Times*. In 2004 I applied for an unpaid leave of absence from the paper. Bob had died in 2003, and I wanted to rest and to spend more time with Conor, who was starting secondary school. Among other things, I needed to step back from the unending flow of breaking stories, to try to analyse events from a different perspective. The news business was changing. Newspaper coverage was being affected by twenty-four-hour TV news networks such as Sky, which were setting the agenda; authors were using their books to break news stories because there was less time for investigative reporting in daily journalism, and satellite television was filled with shouting Americans on Fox News. People were being bombarded with bulletins and alerts at every turn; we were watching TV news in train stations, in hospital, at the gym, in pubs and restaurants, everywhere, without time to reflect on what we were seeing and hearing. Mobile phones were going off at funerals, during concerts and in the middle of plays at the Gate Theatre. Many of us were flirting with meaningless multi-tasking, charging around with MP3 players, Sony Walkmans, portable DVD players, PSPs and BlackBerrys. Pedestrians were crossing busy streets while reading text messages. Drivers were reading text messages while people were crossing busy streets. We were all going around wired up like suicide bombers. It was time, I felt, to turn to the philosophers.

I got my chance about three months later when I attended the publication of *Invoking Ireland* at the Clifden Arts Festival. On a Friday afternoon I left Achill and drove down the coast from Mayo to Galway. I passed through Westport, Carrowkennedy and Leenane, nodding to Killary harbour and the mountains surrounding the fjord. I drove through Letterfrack and Moyard before reaching Clifden, hallowed ground from my Watson Fellowship days. In 1978, when I was packing for Ireland, Tom MacIntyre recommended that I look up Brendan Flynn; he said to inquire in Frank Kelly's bar in Clifden. So that autumn I arrived in Clifden and asked for Frank Kelly's bar, and was directed to a pub on the corner. Two men were sitting with their backs to the bar, facing the door. One looked to be in his forties, amiable and soft-faced; the other man was older, more angular. I approached them.

'Excuse me, I'm looking for Brendan Flynn.'

'Who's looking for him?' the older man demanded.

I was taken aback but stood my ground. I gave him my name, and I said Tom MacIntyre had sent me.

The two men looked at me.

More silence.

Nobody blinked.

'I am Brendan Flynn,' the soft-faced man said, leaning forward slightly on the bar stool.

The older man was Frank Kelly. I laugh to think of it now.

Brendan, from Taugh ma Connell near Ballinasloe, on the Galway-Roscommon border, is a man who loves the arts and artists. He retired in 2005 after thirty-one years as assistant principal of the Clifden Community School; he was acting principal for six of those years. He was a member of the Arts Council from 1998 to 2003. He founded the Clifden Arts Festival in 1977 when the town was a quiet outpost, a destination for discerning French and German holidaymakers and visitors to Inishbofin. It all began with Brendan having poets read to the students in the community school.

Throughout the 1980s I visited Brendan's house overlooking the lake many times en route to Cleggan and Paddy O'Halloran's boat to 'Bofin. There was always someone passing through. Once, in his kitchen, Brendan introduced me to a French ballerina with long blond hair who was living in the area. He mentioned that I had been a newspaper reporter in New York and that I had covered the 'Murder at the Met'. She pouted and said: 'I don't read newz-papers. Zey get my feengeers so dirrr-ty.'

John Moriarty was scheduled to speak at Foyles Hotel, Clifden, on 22 September 2005. The poet Moya Cannon introduced him, praising the intellectual and moral courage of his work in 'an age of new illiteracy'. John stood at the podium bearing the motto: 'The Mind Altering Alters All', and then he began to speak. It was an astonishing performance, a torrent of stories, myths, words and ideas, a verbal concert.

The following morning I interviewed John at Anglers' Return, a guest house four miles from Roundstone and two miles from Ballynahinch Castle, owned and run by Lynn Hill, born Lynette Prynne. Lynn's parents had bought the house in 1954 and turned it into a small, private hotel. After returning from Canada, John lived in a cottage on the property, across the yard, for fourteen years and worked as a gardener. During that time he became close to Lynn, her husband Simon, and their children.

I asked him about what he had stated on Clare Island during our first interview: that *Moby-Dick* was a diagnosis of the western psyche. Could he elaborate?

John replied:

> To me *Moby-Dick* is the finest diagnosis and prognosis that we have of the western psyche in all its historical 'psychles', and I'm saying psychles, not cycles, because I am talking about cultural enactments of psyche. There's the Mesopotamian psychle, the Egyptian psychle, the Greek psychle, the Roman psychle, the medieval Christian psychle, and if you like, Renaissance and modern psychle.
>
> Melville knew, he divined – the great genius will divine things before they are known – that the western psyche was founded on a hatchet job, the hatchet job of killing the dragon in one form or another.
>
> Marduk in Mesopotamia goes out into the abyss and kills Tiamat with her seven heads, so you have a hatchet job in the abyss. In ancient Egypt in the person of the sun-god Atum we went down into the underworld, into our own unconscious, with a spear and there we slaughtered Apophis, the great snake-dragon bellowing at us and hissing at us from the top of his thousand coils.
>
> Now that is a desperate and terrible thing to do. You'll never, ever, ever again be at peace with your own psyche.
>
> You have it in Greece, you have it in Rome, it's right there in Germanic culture. Seamus Heaney has translated *Beowulf*. Beowulf the great hero goes out to kill Grendel. So I'm just saying Melville knew that

we have founded not only our psyches but we have founded our world and our culture on that hatchet job in all and in each and every one of the psychles of western history.

He paused to explain that by using the word diagnosis he meant dia-gnosis, from the Greek 'dia', all the way through, and 'gnosis', to know, meaning to know right through to the core, to the root, of the illness. He pointed out that the *Pequod*, Captain Ahab's ship, was the name of an exterminated Native American tribe.

Now we have Ahab setting out again to repeat the old hatchet job. And this time the beast turns on us, staves us in below waterline, and we go down. And western culture, in Melville's dia-gnosis, is *Pequod* culture, and it's lying below on the floor of the ocean. The culture that gives us our identity, that gives us our meaning, our sense of who we are and who we might be, that culture has already gone to the bottom.

And I am saying I take that diagnosis seriously, and I'm starting at the other side of that collapse, I'm writing for the other side of that collapse. I mightn't be an heir to Melville, but I certainly take up where Melville left off. I accept his dia-gnosis, I accept his prediction, I accept his enactment; he enacted the end of western world culture. That's what *Moby-Dick* does. The ship of western culture has opened at the seams and has taken sinking abyssal water. And it's only Ishmael himself who comes back to tell us what happened.

Western culture in all its psychles is founded on suppression rather than integration. Do you integrate the beast in yourself or do you put your heel on the head of the serpent as Mary does in Catholic iconography? The way of repression and suppression and exclusion hasn't worked for the west because the beast has always been reborn in us. The only way to deal with the beast is to integrate the beast. And Melville knows that, but he didn't for some reason go on to enact it.

Had anyone since Melville tried to integrate the beast?

'Integrating the beast is at the heart of my own literary project,' John said.

How did Melville know all this?

A genius of the exceptional sort that Melville is will intuit this, and he did. A year on board a whaling ship, two years on board the *Acushnet*, which he was, intuitions will come, and he was hugely well read in the Bible and in available world literature.

Melville knew there is that in us which drives us on, he knew that we're self-driven to destruction. And Ahab is the captain, you have the mad captain, the monomaniacal mad captain who hypnotises everyone. Melville's talking about a hypnotised crew, they're hypnotised by this man.

In the chapter called 'The Quarter-deck', they drink Ahab's grog. He says, 'Bring the grog', and all these sailors splice hands on killing the monster. We'll run down this beast and we'll kill him. Then he fills the harpoon sockets with the grog and the harpooners drink from the harpoon sockets, as they would from chalices. Now what kind of Eucharist is that? This is a Black Mass enacted right there. The implication is that in some unconscious sense western culture's been a kind of Black Mass from the word 'go', and that there's an Ahab who's hypnotising us.

Hitler hypnotised all of Germany; did Stalin hypnotise all of Russia? How did people go out and do the terrible things they did? I think society works by hypnosis, not by a conscious social contract.

We all end up quite early in our lives literally hypnotised. How else can I explain people gridlocked in Dublin? How are they willing to do that? Not only to be gridlocked in traffic physically, but to be gridlocked emotionally, intellectually, to be gridlocked, stuck in the traffic of your life, stuck in the traffic of a bad marriage, of a mortgage.

John Moriarty concluded: 'I can only explain modern society in terms of mass hypnosis.'

11

A MID-LIFE BAPTISM IN GALWAY

I lay there, like a chip in the pan, almost twenty years after I had shipped my belongings from New York to Cork, including my oil painting of Sean O'Casey, my Villeroy and Boch porcelain dinner plates with floral pattern, my rocking chair with Williams College insignia, my tape cassette of *Appalachian Spring* by Aaron Copland, my college term paper on *Moby-Dick* entitled 'The Whiteness of the Whale', and forty boxes of other worldly goods and chattel, bound tightly in bubble-packing.

I lay there, in the Galway Clinic, a €100 million private hospital which looked like a lunar-landing spacecraft that had escaped from NASA and perched on the old Dublin Road.

In my spacious two-bedded room I had a few possessions: my travel clock with bell and snooze alarm, my Siemens mobile phone with compact charger, my Philips travel radio with dynamic bass boost and earpiece, my Saturday edition of *The Irish Times,* my unread copy of *The Life of Pi,* basic toiletries and my spiral notebook and pen.

'I'm not going to pat you on the back and tell you you're all right,' Dr Kieran Daly said, when I saw the consultant cardiologist in his rooms in Galway a few days earlier. He was direct but not unkind. He wanted me to have an angiogram, a dye test which outlines the coronary arteries, the blood vessels that bring blood into the muscle of the heart, to see if there were any blockages.

My room-mate in the O'Malley 'pod' in the Galway Clinic

was Sister Anna Flanagan, who had spent forty-three years teaching in the Deep South, most of it in Birmingham, Alabama. She had lived in America longer than I had. Born in Galway city, in a nursing home in Salthill no longer in existence, she grew up in the parish of Aughamore, three miles from Ballyhaunis, County Mayo. Her father, Stanislaus Flanagan, known as Stannie, and her mother, Annie Spelman, were primary school principals. After attending the Convent of Mercy in Roscommon, she wanted to become a nun, but her father suggested she become a teacher first; in hindsight she was grateful for his wisdom. She attended Carysfort teacher-training college in Dublin and became a member of the congregation of the Presentation of the Blessed Virgin Mary.

The America she went to as a young nun was a turbulent place. On 11 June 1963, George Wallace stood in front of a door at the all-white University of Alabama in an attempt to block two black students, Vivian Malone and James Hood, from registering and thereby desegregating the university. Governor Wallace refused to move until he was confronted by federal marshals, the deputy Attorney General of the United States and National Guardsmen. In an act of terrorism in September of that year, Ku Klux Klansmen planted dynamite in the basement of the 16th Street Baptist Church in Birmingham, killing four African-American girls and injuring twenty-two others. In November John F. Kennedy was assassinated in Dallas.

Sister Anna was in her late seventies, retired now and living in the Presentation Convent in Tuam, County Galway. She was in the hospital for an arthroscopy, a knee procedure.

I told her that I was from the Boston area and the subject quickly turned to politics and the failed presidential bid of Senator John Kerry of Massachusetts. It quickly emerged that she wasn't a big fan of George W. Bush, who had been re-elected four months earlier, in November 2004.

'Sister Anna, we are going to get along,' I said.

In November 2000 I had thrown empty Diet Coke cans at the television set in my living room in Achill as the Florida vote went back and forth from Gore to Bush. I dozed off on the couch, thinking Gore had won; when I woke up, Florida had gone to Bush. Wait, no, the American networks weren't sure. Red or blue state, blue or red? In the coming weeks the decision went to the Supreme Court, packed with justices appointed by Bush's father. It was the ballad of the hanging chad. And then something completely un-American happened. The vote-counting was stopped by order of the court. The state of Florida was Pinochet's Chile and the ballots were the new 'disappeared'. For several anxious hours after JFK's assassination in November 1963, my parents had thought there might be a coup d'état. The 2000 presidential election looked like one, too. My mother and father wouldn't recognise the America that was unfolding before my eyes.

My worst fears about Dubya, the most inarticulate US president since his own father, were realised. Trapped at my computer in the newsroom, I watched the bombing of Baghdad in March 2003 live on TV, frozen with shame and remorse. Within hours CNN had taken film footage of the bombing and set it to music. It was *Shock and Awe*: the real-life war movie. I had taken my son to the sites of the D-Day landings in Normandy so that he might develop an appreciation of the scale of sacrifice that had been made by American soldiers during the Second World War, but as I listened to Bush, Cheney, Rumsfeld, Wolfowitz and Rice, and saw the bombs falling on Baghdad, I felt betrayed: America was a long way from Omaha Beach.

In April 2004 President Bush made a visit to the west of Ireland to thank the Irish Government for its 'support' in allowing US planes to land at Shannon. If Bush thought he was coming to Ireland for a photo opportunity with the happy locals, he had misjudged the mood. The abiding image of his trip was the line of tanks deployed to protect him from Irish anti-war protesters at

Dromoland Castle in otherwise peaceful County Clare; the tanks looked like they were heading for Tiananmen Square.

With an estimated 100,000 dead in Iraq by November 2004, the stakes were higher than ever. Suddenly it mattered – to everybody in the world – who was in the White House. I had never seen such international interest in an American presidential election. Even Americans living in Ireland, who tended to be remote from the US political process, were temporarily leaving their families and flying to America to work in 'swing states' for John Kerry. Over the years I had written articles urging Americans in Ireland to send for their absentee ballot papers in order to vote; during this election they didn't need to be reminded.

'You keep bringing up death,' Bush said to Carole Coleman, RTÉ's correspondent, in an interview that irked the White House because she interrupted him. In Bush's world there was war without death: coffins were not allowed to be photographed and civilian casualty numbers were withheld or buried on inside pages of newspapers by headline-grabbing 'terrorist' alerts.

There were US organisations in Ireland, Democrats Abroad and Republicans Abroad, and frequent debates on radio about US foreign policy. As the 2004 Bush versus Kerry election approached, the antipathy towards Bush's foreign policy was so great that Republicans in Ireland stopped going on the radio. One Republican Party spokeswoman in London said it was because they were too busy looking after their businesses. They appeared to be hiding under rocks. At one point I heard a station appeal for any listeners who actually supported Bush to please phone in. An old woman from Cork rang up but it turned out that she wasn't really pro-Bush; she was anti-abortion.

I was asked to go on RTÉ Radio twice in 2004, and both times I criticised President Bush. I wanted people to hear someone with an American accent say that he did not represent the values of all Americans, that no evidence had been found to link Saddam Hussein with the September 11 attacks on New York and

Washington, and that the United Nations' weapons inspectors should have been allowed to finish their work. Tell your friends and relatives in America to vote for John Kerry and give the world a break, I said.

Election Day arrived, 2 November 2004. The votes were cast. An influential pollster predicted a Kerry win. The east coast of America was five hours behind Irish time; I tried to stay up all night for the final result, but fell asleep. The next day Senator Kerry appeared on TV from Faneuil Hall in Boston, tall and Lincolnesque, his voice cracking with disappointment and fatigue. He was conceding.

Apart from the sixty-two million Americans who voted for George Bush (fifty-nine million voted for John Kerry), it seemed as though the rest of the world could not comprehend how such a man could be re-elected President of the United States.

After his victory, the *Guardian* despaired. On the front of an election supplement, in small white letters on a black page, it ran the following headline: 'Oh god'.

'You are a scream,' Sister Anna said, with her left leg stretched out on the bed to ease the pain. She asked me why I was in hospital.

I told her I needed an angiogram. When I googled the term I read that it comes from the Greek word *angeoin*, 'vessel', and *graphien*, 'to write or record'. It was an invasive procedure. A catheter, or tube, was inserted into the femoral artery in the thigh and dye was injected into the catheter.

My difficulties had begun, as many difficulties do, during the *bearna baol*, the gap of danger, the period between 14 December and 14 January when it is particularly dark and dangerous in Ireland, that manic-depressive period consisting of the feverish run-up to Christmas and its anticlimactic aftermath. It was 21 December and we were in the petrol station in Newport, County Mayo, when my mobile rang. It was Assumpta from Mr Kevin Barry's breast clinic in Mayo General Hospital, Castlebar. In a calm, matter-of-fact way, Assumpta told me that the lump in my left breast, detected a year earlier but deemed benign and too small to remove at the time, had grown. The surgical team recommended that it be excised. Mr Barry would perform the procedure in January.

Over the next couple of weeks, as I waited for my hospital appointment, my thoughts turned to my mother, who died of breast cancer on 22 August 1994, and to another Kevin, in Boston, who had helped my family at a difficult time. On the morning after my mother died, the family had said, 'Call Kevin.' They meant Kevin Cullen, a *Boston Globe* reporter who covered the conflict in Northern Ireland. Though he had grown up about two miles from me, in Malden, Massachusetts, we had met in Ireland. He had visited Bob and me in Dalkey in the late 1980s and he'd been quite taken with the idea of our move.

I phoned Kevin and told him that my mother had died. We talked, and after a little while I realised that he was interviewing me. He was taking notes, so I tried to focus. Standing in the room where she had died twelve hours earlier, I described my mother. At one point he said he had to go, that he had to cover a press conference. Then he rang back a short time later, saying his press conference had been cancelled and he had time, so we talked some more. When Kevin was working on a story he was like a good cop, determined and sharp, asking the right questions in a calm manner.

He phoned once or twice more that afternoon to check some facts and get the names of other people to talk to about my mother.

I was awake early the next morning, 23 August 1994, when the *Globe* van drove down Rangeley Road to my sister's house and delivered the paper. It was humid and the house was quiet with sleeping, shocked, bereaved people. I opened the paper, looked at the obituary page, and saw the bylined piece by Kevin Cullen. My mother had the lead obituary in the *Boston Globe:*

Mary Elizabeth Sullivan, 68, former Chelsea school employee

Mary Elizabeth (Hanlon) Sullivan, who worked for the Chelsea School Department for forty-eight years and was one of the last links to the city's old institutions, died yesterday at her daughter's home in Brookline after a long illness. She was sixty-eight.

While thousands of Chelsea natives fled to the suburbs as the old city got poorer, Mrs Sullivan proudly held on.

Her daughter, Sheila Sullivan Lane, a journalist with *The Irish Times* of Dublin, recalled her mother as 'an institution within the city's institutions'.

'The city that my mother came to represent doesn't really exist anymore,' she said. 'The city's in receivership. The schools are being run by Boston University. But to the very end, my mother loved Chelsea. She stood for everything that was good about Chelsea. And she would never leave it.'

Despite the bad press Chelsea frequently gets, friends and family of Mrs Sullivan yesterday said her life stood as testimony to the many good things about Chelsea that don't make the newspapers or the evening news.

Hugh McLaughlin, Chelsea mayor from 1956 to 1960, recalls he grew up with Mrs Sullivan and the man she married, Frederick J. Sullivan, in the section of Chelsea called Ward One.

'She and Fred grew up two streets apart,' said McLaughlin. 'I'm married to the same woman fifty-two years. And it seems like Mary and Fred were always together, too. They were married for thirty-two years before Fred died. I guess we're old-fashioned like that.'

Fred Sullivan eventually became city auditor. Mrs Sullivan, after graduating from Chelsea High School in 1943, attended Boston College and Boston University before launching a career with the school department that spanned a half-century.

Mrs Sullivan sat at the same desk in City Hall for forty-five years. Her longevity was unrivalled. She served as the assistant to School Superintendent Frank Herlihy, and stayed on so long she also served under Herlihy's son, also named Frank, when he became superintendent. She retired in 1990.

Mrs Sullivan was a feminist before the word was coined. 'She was her own person, and she'd stand up to anybody,' McLaughlin recalled.

She was active in Democratic politics, and instilled in her children a sense that politics can work for people who aren't rich or powerful. Her daughter, Kathleen Sullivan Corrigan of Brookline, is an aide to state Senator Thomas Birmingham.

Mrs Sullivan served on the Chelsea Council on Ageing and helped direct the Barnstable Summer Family Theatre on Cape Cod, where she spent her summer vacations.

Besides her daughters, Mrs Sullivan leaves two sons, John F. of Dennis Port, and Frederick J. of Providence; two brothers, Daniel F. Hanlon on Peabody and John J. Hanlon of Chelsea; and four grandchildren, Conor Lane of Dublin and Matthew, Patrick and Megan Corrigan of Brookline.

Kevin had described a person whom he had never met and in doing so, had recreated the life of a city.

To the right of my mother's obituary was that of Catholicos Vazgen I, patriarch of the Armenian Apostolic Church, aged eighty-five. The headlines on the obituaries were the same size, but my mother's obit was four hundred and seventy-six words long and the patriarch's was four hundred and twenty.

Recalling the events years later I said to Kevin, 'An Irish matriarch beat the Armenian patriarch for the lead obituary.'

He responded: 'I'm sure Armenians in Watertown saw this and said, "Ah, sure, the Irish take care of their own, don't they?"'

In 1997 Kevin opened the *Globe's* Dublin bureau, achieving a long-held ambition. He closed it in 1998 when he was promoted to chief European correspondent and moved to London, although he had fought hard to stay in Ireland. In 2001 he returned to Boston and joined the investigative team that broke open the child sexual abuse scandal in the Catholic Church, for which the *Globe* received the 2003 Pulitzer Prize for Public Service. The investigative team worked on nothing other than the abuse story for nearly two years. When I asked Kevin about the coverage and the effect it had on Cardinal Bernard Law of Boston, he said:

> Certainly the coverage was the catalyst for Law's departure. The Attorney General (of Massachusetts), Tom Reilly, whose parents were from Ireland, would not have investigated Law if not for the stories. I think, though, the real reason Law left was not because he faced potential prosecution, but because he had lost the ability to lead: he had no moral authority, and donations to the Church were down markedly. The Vatican realised the archdiocese, already facing serious financial difficulties, would go into bankruptcy if Law, the boil, was not lanced. So they gave him a nice sinecure in Rome, in charge of one of the seven important chapels there.

More than ten years after my mother's death, the date for my own breast surgery was set: 20 January 2005, my father's birthday and the inauguration day of the re-elected US president. Bush's inauguration was live on Sky television in the operating theatre. Mr Barry, consultant general and breast surgeon, who had spent two years of his surgical training at Johns Hopkins in Baltimore, Maryland, and another year working in surgical training at the Mayo Clinic in Rochester, Minnesota, greeted me warmly. A Limerick man, he was soft-spoken, focused, authoritative and calm, with dark brown hair and an unhurried bedside manner. We were lucky to have him in Castlebar. The anaesthetist, whom I didn't know, was brisk. He asked me if I was wearing dentures. I said no. God almighty, did I look old enough to be wearing dentures? Bush was raising his right hand while Laura Bush looked adoringly at him. The anaesthetist said something to me about the inauguration. The last thing I remember telling him was, 'I oppose the policies of George Bush,' before he knocked me out.

When I woke up that evening, they said that Mr Barry had been pleased. It looked like a benign fibroadenoma; he had excised all of it using the technique of wire-guided localisation and excision biopsy, and the results would be back in a few weeks. I was deeply relieved. The anaesthetist, however, was not totally satisfied. He had noted ectopic heartbeats, extra beats, on my electrocardiogram during the procedure, and they needed to be checked out. There had been a lot of ectopics, as the medical staff called them. 'You may need an angiogram,' Mr Barry told me the next morning.

In the following days I learned that caffeine and stress were two possible causes of ectopic heartbeats. The Web was full of people who had them and in many cases they were benign. My stress test results were good and my blood pressure and cholesterol levels were normal. I resisted the angiogram.

'Can't I walk, eliminate caffeine and see what happens?' I asked Dr Daly at our first appointment in Galway.

That's when he said, 'I'm not going to pat you on the back and tell you you're all right.' He was a tall and spare man, with white hair and a neat white beard. There was a hint of humour in his stern gaze.

'When can you do it?' I asked. It was Friday 4 March 2005. I told him I had health insurance.

He looked down at his desk. 'On Monday in the Galway Clinic.' Normally I would applaud efficiency in the health service, but in this case I hated it.

I broke the news to Brent and Conor in the waiting room. Brent was leaning forward and Conor's brown eyes were opened wide. He didn't blink.

I was afraid but tried not to show it. I already expected the worst, that I would need drugs or more surgery, that at the very least my life would change profoundly, that I might not be headed to a ripe old age. Would I become an invalid? Would I be unable to work? I was forty-eight. Conor was only thirteen.

'I'll say a rosary for you,' Sister Anna said.

I lay back on the hospital bed and closed my eyes.

On the night before my angiogram I paced the corridors of the Galway Clinic. The night nurse looked at me with concern. I repeatedly rang home to Achill on my mobile. Conor had missed school to come with Brent and me to Galway and he was having trouble finding out what his homework assignments were; it epitomised the powerlessness of my situation.

I returned to my hospital bed and looked at the calendar. The angiogram was scheduled for the next day, 7 March, the day before the anniversary of my father's death. Somehow my medical problems with breast and heart had occurred between the two poles of the dates of his birth and death.

When I checked into the Galway Clinic, I had asked out of curiosity if the hospital had a religious ethos. 'Non-denominational,' the young woman in the admissions office said.

There was a crucifix on the wall of my hospital room, and I was glad it was there. At such times I found it hard to be agnostic.

I tried to put the paedophile priest scandal out of my mind, and the Catholic Church in general. I tried to separate what faith I still clung to from the tragically-flawed institution. I prayed in my own way and I appealed to my father, dead these past twenty-four years. I need some help here, Dad.

That evening a small priest with a round face rushed into the hospital room carrying a cup or vessel of some kind. I liked his sense of purpose and determination. His mission was to minister to the sick; he didn't chat, he didn't intrude and he didn't ask questions. He didn't ask whether I was a practising Catholic or if I had read *The Da Vinci Code*. He didn't care what my views were on women priests (in favour) or mandatory celibacy for priests (against). He was a non-judgmental foot soldier of the Church. I realised as he got closer to me that he had come to give out Communion, and before you could say *Urbi et Orbi* he had popped a host in my mouth. He gave Communion to Sister Anna and left our hospital room as quickly and mysteriously as he had appeared. She murmured her thanks while I lay there in silence. I had run dry on words and at last I fell asleep.

Unbeknownst to me, Sister Anna had been thinking about my plight, about the death of my former husband and my possible heart condition. She was about the same age as my mother would have been if she had lived, and her attitude from the moment of my admission to hospital had been maternal. Aware of my distress and outraged that my son should be confronted with the spectre of something happening to his remaining biological parent, she had decided to do something about it herself. She said a rosary and she had all the sisters in the convent pray for me. And then she got her bottle of holy water and put it beside her mobile phone, which she had smuggled into her bed under the covers. With all the patience and fortitude of a nun who had survived George Wallace and the Ku Klux Klan, she lay in wait for me.

The next morning, as the nurses came to take me down for the procedure, Sister Anna was ready. 'Good luck,' she said quietly. 'I said a rosary for you.' The nurses who were pushing my trolley slowed down as we approached her bed. I looked at Sister Anna. She was holding a bottle of holy water in her left hand. Then, to my astonishment, she started winding up her right arm, her throwing arm, like a relief pitcher for the Red Sox, and she began flinging holy water at me. She was gentle at first, sprinkling me, but as I passed by she became more vehement. As I was passing beyond her reach, she flung the entire contents of the bottle at me, her face tight with concentration as the holy water splashed on my face and neck. As she threw that final mighty pitch, she winced at the pain in her knee. She should be a priest, I thought.

The nurses wheeled me downstairs and I waited for my angiogram. There were a few patients in front of me, all of them older men. We lay there on our trolleys, stacked up like airplanes on a runway. The nurses were chatty and upbeat; several had lived in the US and had come back to Ireland during the economic boom. Soon it was my turn to leave the runway.

'It's a pity we don't have some of Brent's music,' Dr Daly said kindly before he began.

'Yes,' I murmured. My thoughts drifted to Brent, from Christchurch, New Zealand, who was minding Conor. Brent had gone to the US for the first time in the late 1990s and visited Cape Cod with me. We stood before a sign that said First Encounter Beach, where the Pilgrims were driven back by hostile Native Americans in 1620. The Native Americans were right, of course. Wouldn't you be hostile if you saw a shipload of Pilgrims heading towards your tranquil beach?

'Where are the Indians?' Brent had asked.

Where were the Indians indeed?

Dr Daly made a tiny puncture in the femoral artery in my upper right thigh and inserted a catheter. I closed my eyes. I felt pressure but no pain. The theatre was cold and everybody was wearing what looked like green bullet-proof vests. He injected some dye.

A short time later, Dr Daly said, 'Look at that.'

I froze and refused to look at the screen.

'Look at *what*?' I snapped.

A couple of excruciatingly long seconds passed. Then he said: 'Clean as a whistle. Like a newborn baby's.'

He meant my arteries. There were no blockages, not even the faintest hint of one.

I sighed and looked at the X-ray on the screen as a tear ran down my right cheek. I glanced at my angiogram result. It looked like a weather map of clouds over Ireland.

'See?' Dr Daly asked helpfully, but I could not focus on the screen. He was smiling. I thought briefly of the men outside on the trolleys who were still waiting for their tests. How many would get a bill of health like that?

'Clean as a whistle, like a newborn baby's' was the one result I had not expected. I shed more tears of relief and, after a while, the nurses brought me back to my room and pulled the curtain around my bed. They instructed me to lie flat on my back for four hours while the wound in my right thigh clotted. Do not lift your head for any reason, they said.

I lay there and reflected on my reprieve. As I saw it, the tables had turned in my favour when Sister Anna Flanagan from County Mayo performed my mid-life baptism in Galway.

'Are you still here?' Dr Daly asked wryly a few hours later.

Funny guy. Another tear rolled down my cheek.

'You can go home now.' No medication, no further treatment, watch the caffeine and walk. 'See how you get on.'

'That sounded good,' Sister Anna called out after Dr Daly had gone.

She had been eavesdropping intently in the next bed behind the curtain and, despite being groggy and in pain from her own knee operation, she was extremely pleased. 'Now,' she said.

Her work done, she fell asleep, and Brent arrived to take me home to Conor in Achill.